The Quest for Shakespeare's Garden

Written by ROY STRONG

with illustrations from the collections of the
Shakespeare Birthplace Trust

I know a bank where the wild thyme blows . . .

Shakespeare
birthplace trust

Thames & Hudson

Sir Roy Strong is an art historian, museum curator, writer, broadcaster and landscape designer. He has served as director of both the National Portrait Gallery and the Victoria and Albert Museum in London. Strong, who was knighted in 1982, was made a Companion of Honour in 2016. He is also an honorary fellow of the Shakespeare Birthplace Trust.

Frontispiece: Detail of *The Bust of Shakespeare Encircled by All the Flowers Mentioned in his Works*, Clara Maria Pope, *c.* 1835

Quotation on page 3: Oberon, *A Midsummer Night's Dream*, Act 2, Scene 1

For information on the sources of the engravings and decorative details used throughout the book, see page 109.

First published in the United Kingdom in 2016 by
Thames & Hudson Ltd, 181A High Holborn, London WC1V 7QX

Published in association with the Shakespeare Birthplace Trust

The Quest for Shakespeare's Garden © 2016 Thames & Hudson Ltd, London

Text © 2016 Sir Roy Strong

British Library Cataloguing-in-Publication Data
A catalogue record for this book is available from the British Library

ISBN 978-0-500-25224-6

Printed and bound in China by C & C Offset Printing Co. Ltd

To find out about all our publications, please visit
www.thamesandhudson.com. There you can subscribe to
our e-newsletter, browse or download our current catalogue,
and buy any titles that are in print.

CONTENTS

FOREWORD
by the Shakespeare Birthplace Trust

William Shakespeare has long been associated with nature, and his plays and poems are full of references to the flowers, herbs and trees that he knew and saw in the world around him. Today, visitors to the five family homes associated with Shakespeare in Stratford-upon-Avon experience five very different gardens – living, breathing spaces that afford us a very real link to Shakespeare's works and his world. Although Shakespeare's final home, New Place, is no longer standing, records show that there has been a garden on the site of New Place in some form for over 400 years.

Fittingly, while we were preparing this book, the Trust's garden team was laying out a new garden at New Place to commemorate the 400th anniversary of Shakespeare's death. The new space marries contemporary landscapes and sculptures with the traditional features of an Elizabethan garden. One notable feature is that the knot garden originally created for the Trust by historian Ernest Law in the 1920s has been replanted.

It is this knot garden that is at the centre of *The Quest for Shakespeare's Garden*, and who better to recount its story and its place in garden history than Sir Roy Strong, pre-eminent art historian and writer on the English Renaissance, garden historian – and garden maker – and a fellow of the Shakespeare Birthplace Trust.

Law drew on authentic Elizabethan sources for his knot garden design, and here we have drawn inspiration from the same original sources and the wonderful selection of materials relating to Shakespeare and gardens in the Trust's rich collections.

Opposite Detail of embroidered 'sweet' bag, 1575–1600, showing the Elizabethans' love of pattern and design based on the natural world

Overleaf The knot garden at New Place was designed by Ernest Law, a trustee of the Shakespeare Birthplace Trust, and opened to great acclaim in 1920.

It standeth north-north-east and by east fro

INTRODUCTION

I first visited the garden of Shakespeare's house New Place in Stratford-upon-Avon in 1954, when, as a young student, I had come to see the plays. I was already fired with a love of the Elizabethan age and on a trajectory that would lead to a series of books and articles on the portraiture and pageantry of the era. Gardening was to form no part of that passion until, in the 1970s together with my late wife, the designer Julia Trevelyan Oman, we began to plant a major garden. Suddenly I became obsessed by the history of gardening, discovering that no one had as yet written a properly documented account of gardens and gardening in Tudor and early Stuart England. The result was the book *The Renaissance Garden in England* (1979) which appeared the same year that the exhibition 'The Garden' was staged at the Victoria and Albert Museum, London, of which I was director.

he weſt corner of thy curiouſ-knotted garden.

KING, *LOVE'S LABOUR'S LOST*, ACT I, SCENE I

At that date garden history was still a new and exciting academic subject. In 1965 The Garden History Society (now The Garden Trust) was launched and garden history began to take off. By the middle of the 1980s it had become a university subject, and garden archaeology, conservation and restoration were also beginning to burgeon. The result has been a steady stream of major books and articles up to the present day, covering every aspect of the history of the garden in Britain.

This is the background that led to my quest for Shakespeare's own garden. The subject arose out of a lecture I gave on the subject at the Folger Shakespeare Library, Washington, DC, in 1991. The story of the New Place garden is an extraordinary one, bringing onto the stage a most unlikely cast of characters, including E. F. Benson, the novelist; Daisy, Countess of Warwick, mistress to Edward VII; another novelist, the notorious Marie Corelli; and the historian of Hampton Court Palace, Ernest Law. As I pieced together the story of the recreation of the New Place garden, I began to realize its importance as a seminal document in both the emergence of garden history and garden recreation. Meanwhile the phenomenon of creating what are called 'Shakespeare gardens' began to proliferate across the globe. But let me now begin this remarkable story by ushering onto the stage the first of my unlikely cast of characters, E. F. Benson's Lucia Lucas.

Benson's Lucia novels are among my favourite reading, wicked satires of English provincial life between the two world wars. The heroine, if she can be designated as such, Lucia Lucas, is a woman prone to misplaced cultural pretensions. The plots centre on her battle with the formidable Miss Mapp for the domination of the village of Tilling, based on Rye in Sussex where Benson lived and, indeed, was mayor from 1934 to 1937. With characteristic malice, in *Queen Lucia*, published in 1920, he describes Lucia's house, The Hurst in Riseholme, where she lived before

Opposite The title page of Ernest Law's *Shakespeare's Garden*, 1922, illustrating the four original Elizabethan knot designs that inspired New Place garden

Left Detail from the title page of John Gerard's *The Herball*, 1633 edition

SHAKESPEARE'S GARDEN

STRATFORD-UPON-AVON

By ERNEST LAW, C.B.

ONE OF THE TRUSTEES

WITH ILLUSTRATIONS

LONDON:

SELWYN & BLOUNT, LTD.

21, YORK BUILDINGS, ADELPHI, W.C.2

1922

moving to Tilling, as three sixteenth-century cottages knocked into one and done over, in the author's words, 'a shade more blatantly Elizabethan than the stem onto which it was grafted'. In this stage set Lucia would indulge in the affectation of strumming at the virginals and looking out on to her garden, which Benson describes, in the following terms:

HERE, as was only right and proper, there was not a flower to be found save such as were in the plays of Shakespeare: indeed, it was called Shakespeare's garden, and the bed that ran below the windows of the dining-room was Ophelia's border, for it consisted solely of those flowers which that distraught maiden distributed to her friends when she should have been in a lunatic asylum. Mrs. Lucas often reflected how lucky it was that such institutions were unknown in Elizabeth's day. Pansies, naturally, formed the chief decoration (though there were some very flourishing plants of rue) and Mrs. Lucas always wore a bunch of them when in flower, to inspire her thoughts, and found them wonderfully efficacious. Round the sundial, which was set in the middle of one of the squares of grass between which a path of broken paving-stones led to the front door, was a circular border, now, in July, sadly vacant, for it harboured only the spring flowers enumerated by Perdita. But the first day every year when Perdita's border put forth its earliest blossom was a delicious anniversary, and the news of it spread like wildfire through Mrs. Lucas's kingdom, and her subjects were very joyful, and came to salute the violet or daffodil, or whatever it was.

Therewith fantastic garlands did she make

Crowflowers

Daisies

Of crow-flowers, nettles, daisies, and long purples

QUEEN GERTRUDE, *HAMLET*, ACT 4, SCENE 7

The actress Jane Lessingham played Ophelia in a production of *Hamlet* at the Covent Garden Theatre in 1772. Her flower-strewn dress and loose-flowing hair illustrate distraught Ophelia's words, 'There's rue for you' (Act 4, Scene 5).

Here's flowers for you:
Hot lavender, mints, savory, marjoram,
The marigold. . .These are flowers
Of middle summer. . .

PERDITA, *THE WINTER'S TALE*, ACT 4, SCENE 4

There's no sign here of any attempt at recreating an Elizabethan knot garden, but Lucia fills her garden with flowers mentioned in the plays. She calls it a Shakespeare garden. Benson, ever up-to-the-minute with his biting social satire, could only have had in mind what was going on in Stratford-upon-Avon that year. Amid a blaze of publicity, the Birthplace Trustees had authorized their newest recruit, the historian Ernest Law (1854–1930), to design and plant a historically accurate garden such as Shakespeare would have recognized.

Benson was to return to the subject of the Queen of Riseholme's Shakespeare garden eleven years later in *Mapp and Lucia* (1931). Here he provides a more detailed description of it:

> IT was a charming little square plot in front of the timbered facade of the Hurst, surrounded by yew hedges and intersected with paths of crazy pavement, carefully smothered in stone-crop, which led to the Elizabethan sundial from Wardour Street in the centre. It was gay in spring with those flowers (and no others) on which Perdita doted. There were 'violets dim,' and primroses and daffodils, which came before the swallow dared and took the winds (usually of April) with beauty. But now in June the swallow had dared long ago, and when spring and the daffodils were over, Lucia always allowed Perdita's garden a wider, though still strictly Shakespearean scope. There was eglantine (Penzance briar) in full flower now, and honeysuckle and gillyflowers and plenty of pansies for thoughts, and yards of rue (more than usual this year), and so Perdita's garden was gay all the summer.

Gillyflowers

Opposite The Shepherd's Cot with Florizel, Perdita, a shepherd, a clown, Mopsa, servants, Polixenes and Camillo, disguised. Detail of an engraving by J. Fittler after a painting by F. Wheatley, RA

Benson was nothing if not a keen social satirist. This time he was a little more wicked, for Wardour Street was notorious for selling fake antiques. But we now learn that the Shakespeare garden was square, enclosed by a yew hedge, and had intersecting paths of crazy paving. This time more flowers are listed: daffodils, violets, primroses, eglantine, honeysuckle, gillyflowers and rue. Somewhat surprisingly, rosemary has vanished.

The type of garden he is describing with its sundial, crazy-paving paths, yew hedging and herbs is, in terms of design and planting, a between-the-wars suburban descendant of the Arts and Crafts garden style, the iconic creators of which were Gertrude Jekyll (1843–1932) and William Robinson (1838–1935) at the close of the nineteenth century. The new style became popular in reaction to the apotheosis of bedding out hundreds of brightly coloured annuals, originating from South America, in rigid patterns. Under the aegis of that great plantswoman Jekyll, this style focused instead on the deployment of native plants arranged in painterly borders set within a structure that made use of natural materials like stone and wood for paths and pergolas. The great gardens that Jekyll worked on with the architect Sir Edwin Lutyens (1869–1944) were the apogee of this style, typified by one of their masterpieces, Hestercombe in Somerset.

Illustration from the introduction to Henry Ellacombe's
The Plant-Lore and Garden-Craft of Shakespeare, 1896 edition

But there's more to Benson's satire than this, as he was notorious for basing his female characters on well-known public figures. For the flamboyant and outrageous Lucia, he certainly drew on the popular novelist Marie Corelli (1855–1924). What was more, Marie Corelli actually lived in Shakespeare's Stratford-upon-Avon. She had begun in 1899 by renting properties there, and then purchased a dilapidated mansion called Mason Croft, casting herself shortly after as Shakespeare's chief custodian. Although as a character virtually impossible (she was loathed by most of the 'powers that be' in the town), she bestowed a large part of her wealth to ensure that what was left of the playwright's town was not swept away. Indeed, just a few years before her death, she had saved the day by contributing a cheque for £50 towards the planting of Ernest Law's New Place garden. That garden was planted after a major public appeal and amid a barrage of publicity during the winter of 1919 to 1920.

Marie Corelli was also flower-obsessed, her house fairly dripping with window boxes stuffed with flowers. Being short, fat and utterly fulfilling Lady Bracknell's description of Miss Prism as 'a female of repellent aspect' in no way deterred the unsinkable novelist from attending the Shakespeare Festival of 1902 dressed as a pansy, her bosom encased in two gargantuan ones, sporting a pansy headdress and carrying a basket of them. At sixty-five she staged a Daffodil Dance with the walls of her music room banked four feet high with daffodils.

The absurdity of both these women does, however, raise the serious question of precisely when did the plants and flowers referred to in Shakespeare's works assume a cult status, which graduated to a campaign to reinstate a garden of the kind that the playwright would have recognized for New Place, the house in which he died in 1616. Who first planted a Shakespeare garden? Who first attempted to recreate an Elizabethan knot garden? This quest is a fundamental one, for in pursuing it we are tapping not only into the origins of what was to burgeon into the academic discipline of garden history in our era but also into the first attempt to do something with which we are now all too familiar: to restore or recreate historic gardens. The garden of New Place is in fact the crucial matrix, for its creation in the years immediately after the First World War was the culmination of a whole complex of strands stretching back to the beginning of the nineteenth century and earlier. And it is to an exploration of these that I will now turn.

Pray, love, remember. And there is pansies; that's for thoughts.

OPHELIA, *HAMLET*, ACT 4, SCENE 5

Opposite Marie Corelli in her pansy costume at Mason Croft, 1902

Wild pansies

SHAKESPEARE & THE WORLD OF NATURE

MUCH of Shakespeare's use of plants and flowers in his plays is as emblems. In this he closely reflects the thought context of the period. His was the age of the emblem book, when the whole of the visible world was symbolically codified and could, by the educated classes, be read. The Virgin Queen surrounded herself with a web of virginal floral imagery from the eglantine to the pansy, one that we can trace not only in literary tributes but also in the embroidery on the dresses in her vast wardrobe.

In the playwright's case, such an approach is neatly demonstrated in one of the most famous of all symbolic plant references in the plays, that

Above Detail of an embroidered silk pillow depicting tulips, roses and irises, 1600s
Opposite Detail of a richly embroidered bodice made of fine linen reflecting the wearer's wealth and status, early seventeenth century

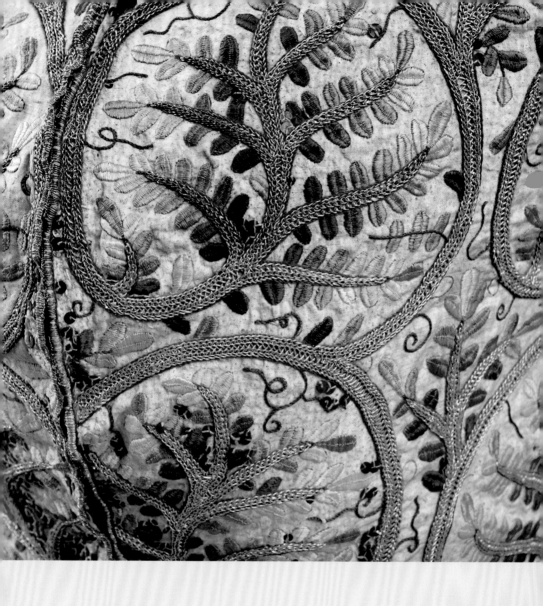

In em'rald tufts, flowers purple, blue, and white,
Like sapphire, pearl, and rich embroidery,
Buckled below fair knighthood's bending knee—
Fairies use flowers for their charactery.

MISTRESS QUICKLY, *THE MERRY WIVES OF WINDSOR*, ACT 5, SCENE 5

Whisper her ear, and tell her I and Ursula
Walk in the orchard, and our whole discourse
Is all of her. Say that thou overheard'st us,
And bid her steal into the pleachèd bower
Where honeysuckles, ripened by the sun,
Forbid the sun to enter. . .

HERO, *MUCH ADO ABOUT NOTHING*, ACT 3, SCENE I

in the mad scene in *Hamlet*, when Ophelia utters: *'There's rosemary, that's for remembrance. Pray, love, remember. . .There's fennel for you and columbines'* (Act 4, Scene 5). References in other plays fill this out. The events in *A Midsummer Night's Dream*, for example, hinge on the juice of the *Viola tricolor*, which is given the power to engender love on first sight when applied to the eyes:

> . . .*a little western flower* —
> *Before, milk-white; now purple with love's wound* —
> *And maidens call it 'love-in-idleness'.*
>
> OBERON, *A MIDSUMMER NIGHT'S DREAM*, ACT 2, SCENE I

Above Finely embroidered cuff of a man's kid glove, early seventeenth century
Opposite Orchard scene from *Much Ado About Nothing*, with Hero, Ursula and Beatrice.
Detail of an engraving by P. Simon after a painting by Rev. W. Peters, RA

The *Winter's Tale*, one of Shakespeare's last and most plant-filled plays, has in Perdita's speech a cascade of the flowers that would have figured in a grand Elizabethan garden in spring.

> . . .*O Proserpina,*
> *For the flowers now that, frighted, thou letst fall*
> *From Dis's wagon! — daffodils,*
> *That come before the swallow dares, and take*
> *The winds of March with beauty; violets, dim,*
> *But sweeter than the lids of Juno's eyes*
> *Or Cytherea's breath; pale primroses,*
> *That die unmarried ere they can behold*
> *Bright Phoebus in his strength — a malady*
> *Most incident to maids; bold oxlips, and*
> *The crown imperial; lilies of all kinds,*
> *The flower-de-luce being one.*
>
> PERDITA, *THE WINTER'S TALE*, ACT 4, SCENE 4

Two centuries later, mentions such as these inspired a flood of books on the plants and flowers to be found in Shakespeare's plays.

But to them we can add another, perhaps more telling, reference, the image of the kingdom as a garden. Shakespeare gives that notion its most enduring expression in *Richard II*, when a gardener instructs his two assistants to '*Cut off the heads of too fast growing sprays / That look too lofty in our commonwealth*'. They then complain about the task:

> *When our sea-wallèd garden, the whole land,*
> *Is full of weeds, her fairest flowers choked up,*
> *Her fruit trees all unpruned, her hedges ruined,*
> *Her knots disordered, and her wholesome herbs*
> *Swarming with caterpillars?*
>
> MAN, *RICHARD II*, ACT 3, SCENE 4

Opposite above Two gardeners at work in Thomas Hill's *The Gardeners Labyrinth*, 1577

Opposite below Decoration on the title page of William Lawson's *The Country Housewife's Garden*, 1648 edition

. . . .the whole land, Is full of weeds. . .

MAN, *RICHARD II*, ACT 3, SCENE 4

To the great Variety of Readers.

FRom the moſt able, to him that can but ſpell: Th
you are number'd. We had rather you were weig
Eſpecially, when the fate of all Bookes depends
on your capacities : and not of your heads alor
but of your purſes. Well ! It is now publique, & y
wil ſtand for your priuiledges wee know : to re:
and cenſure. Do ſo, but buy it firſt. That doth b
commend a Booke, the Stationer ſaies. Then, how odde ſoeuer yc
braines be, or your wiſedomes, make your licence the ſame, and ſp:
not. Iudge your ſixe-pen'orth, your ſhillings worth, your fiue ſl
lings worth at a time, or higher, ſo you riſe to the iuſt rates, and w
come. But, what euer you do, Buy. Cenſure will not driue a Tra
or make the Iacke go. And though you be a Magiſtrate of wit, and
on the Stage at *Black-Friers,* or the *Cock-pit,* to arraigne Playes dail
know, theſe Playes haue had their triall alreadie, and ſtood out all A
peales ; and do now come forth quitted rather by a Decree of Cou
then any purchas'd Letters of commendation.

It had bene a thing, we confeſſe, worthie to haue bene wiſhed, tl
the Author himſelfe had liu'd to haue ſet forth, and ouerſeen his ow
writings ; But ſince it hath bin ordain'd otherwiſe, and he by death c
parted from that right, we pray you do not envie his Friends, the off.
of their care, and paine, to haue collected & publiſh'd them ; and ſo
haue publiſh'd them, as where (before) you were abus'd with diue
ſtolne, and ſurreptitious copies, maimed, and deformed by the frau
and ſtealthes of iniurious impoſtors, that expos'd them : euen tho
are now offer'd to your view cur'd, and perfect of their limbes ; and
the reſt, abſolute in their numbers, as he conceiued thē. Who, as he v
a happie imitator of Nature, was a moſt gentle expreſſer of it. His m
and hand went together : And what he thought, he vttered with tl
eaſineſſe, that wee haue ſcarſe receiued from him a blot in his pap

The equation of England and a garden was inevitable with the accession of a dynasty, the Tudors, whose symbol was the union of two roses. Gardens appear in the queen's portraits, and gardens figured too in the courtly pageantry that welcomed her on progress. The image of the garden as the kingdom continued with the Stuarts. An arch described as 'The Garden of Plenty' welcomed James I on his entry into London in 1604, and flower-bedecked gardens recur time and again as images of the kingdom in the great series of court masques down to the Civil War. Andrew Marvell's poem 'Upon Appleton House, to my Lord Fairfax', written during the Commonwealth, sees that benign image suddenly destroyed: '*Oh thou, That dear and happy Isle / The Garden of the World ere while. . .*'

Even during the reign of Edward VII (r. 1901–10), Rudyard Kipling, in his 'The Glory of the Garden', includes the reiterated line '*Our England is a garden*'. And so the seeds of all that was to happen and stimulate the desire to recreate an Elizabethan garden were there from the start, awaiting the appropriate moment to spring to life.

That moment would come with the Romantic movement's cult of Nature and Shakespeare's role as its supreme poet. The latter can be traced all the way back to the introductory pages of the 1623 folio of his works in which he was constituted above all as the literary exemplar of Nature in contrast to Ben Jonson, a master of Art. In the introduction he was billed as 'a happie imitator of Nature'. During the seventeenth century that role was to tell against Shakespeare: being regarded as a rough, unpolished Poet of Nature, it was only right that what were then seen as the uncouth aspects of his work should be cut or recast to accord with the ideals of a more classically minded and refined age. All of that changed in the middle of the eighteenth century, when Augustan order with its appeal to the intellect, gave way to the challenge of a response through the passions.

Above Ornament from the title page of *The Gardeners Labyrinth*, 1577
Opposite Introductory page from the First Folio of Shakespeare's works, 1623

In this new ideological context Shakespeare's ascent to divinity may seem inevitable, but it was to a very large extent owed to one man, the actor David Garrick (1717–79). He deliberately set out to cast himself in duality with the poet and, in 1769, staged a three-day Jubilee in his honour at Stratford-upon-Avon. The climax was Garrick unveiling a statue of the bard, which he presented to the town and in front of which he declaimed his own verses eulogizing

> . . .that demi-god!
> Who Avon's flow'ry margin trod,
> While sportive Fancy round him flew,
> Where Nature led him by the hand,
> Instructed him in all she knew,
> And gave him absolute command!

In 1757 a critic wrote that in Garrick 'a great genius hath arisen to dignify the stage, who, when it was sinking in the lowest insipidity, restored it to the fullness of its ancient splendour, and, with a variety of powers beyond example, established *Nature, Shakespeare* and *himself. . .*' After his retirement in 1776, the actor was presented with an enamelled medallion which literally depicts what the critic wrote. On its surface, we see Garrick attired as a classical actor wearing a toga and clasping the masks of tragedy and comedy. He is unveiling a herm, out of which springs the weird combination of Shakespeare and the goddess Nature in the form of the many-breasted Ephesian Diana. Shakespeare points to his own head to indicate that he depends for his genius on his fertile partner, Nature. The scene was set for the following century to explore the implications of this recasting of the playwright.

Where Nature led him by the hand. . . And gave him absolute command!

DAVID GARRICK, 1769

Opposite David Garrick, Robert Edge Pine, *c.* 1770
Oil on canvas, 114 × 75 cm (44⅞ × 29½ in.)
A copy of the lost Gainsborough portrait destroyed by fire in 1946

We can take this visual expression of Shakespeare and Nature further with a painting by George Romney (1734–1802) of *Nature unveiling herself to the Infant Shakespeare*. It was inspired by a passage in Thomas Gray's *The Progress of Poesy* (c. 1753):

> *Far from the sun and summer-gale,*
> *In thy green lap was Nature's darling laid,*
> *What time, where lucid Avon strayed,*
> *To him the mighty mother did unveil*
> *Her awful face: the dauntless child*
> *Stretched forth his little arms, and smiled.*

The oil painting, which no longer exists, was begun in the middle of the 1780s and was never finished, but a cartoon and several sketches survive. In these the kneeling figure of Nature, in the form of a classical female figure, lifts a veil from the sleeping infant poet in his cradle. There is no sign yet of so much as a flower garland. But, as the worship of the playwright as an elemental force of Nature, and therefore above all rules, entered its Romantic heyday, that would inevitably come.

What both the medallion and the picture signal is the visualization of Shakespeare's dramatic works by painters. This occurred in the long series of paintings commissioned by Alderman John Boydell for his Shakespeare Gallery, which opened in Pall Mall to the public in 1789, the year the French Revolution broke out. Boydell was a prosperous publisher of prints, who commissioned the leading artists of the day to paint scenes from the plays that were then engraved. The hundred paintings he commissioned and eventually, in 1803, issued in one huge folio volume are a keen index of Shakespeare's domination of the Romantic imagination and of the poet's increasing centrality in terms of national identity during a period when the country was at war with France. Boydell was not the first person to present an illustrated Shakespeare: starting with Nicholas Rowe's edition of the plays in 1709, they were available throughout the eighteenth century. No other series, however, was attended by such a blaze of publicity or were so widely known; the gallery itself was open to visitors for a decade and a half and separate prints were widely available for

Overleaf Scene in the Temple Garden with the Earls of Somerset, Suffolk and Warwick, Richard Plantagenet, Vernon and another lawyer. *Henry VI, Part 1*, Act 2, Scene 4. Engraving by John Ogborne after a painting by J. Boydell

framing in their own right. Here, within the scenes chosen, we see virtually all the key passages in which flowers figure in a major way in the plays. The folio of 1803 opens with a print after another composition by George Romney entitled *The Infant Shakespeare attended by Nature and the Passions*; Francis Wheatley (1747–1801) depicts Perdita with her spring flowers from *The Winter's Tale* (see page 14); Boydell himself renders the famous scene in the Temple Garden when the rival dynasties chose the white and the red roses of York and Lancaster (overleaf); and Benjamin West catches the demented Ophelia proffering her rosemary for remembrance.

The Infant Shakspeare attended by Nature and the Passions
Engraving by Benjamin Smith after a painting by George Romney

Nature is represented with her face unveiled to her favourite Child, who is placed between Joy and Sorrow. To the right of Nature are Love, Hatred and Jealousy: to her left, Anger, Envy and Fear.

Prick not your finger as you pluck it o

st, bleeding, you do paint the white rose red.

SOMERSET, *HENRY VI, PART I*, ACT 2, SCENE 4

With these scenes in mind and the arrival of what is known as the language of flowers in the 1830s (to which I will come in the next chapter), the progression towards assembling the poet's blossoms into one composition was but a short step. That step was taken by the flower painter Clara Maria Pope (1767–1838) who, in 1835, exhibited in the Royal Academy a picture entitled *The Bust of Shakespeare Encircled by all the Flowers Mentioned in his Works*. Mrs Pope taught at the Royal Academy, and her first husband was the painter Francis Wheatley, for whom she had acted as a model for some of the prettier figures in his famous series, the 'Cries of London'. She herself was a highly accomplished botanical painter. She was also a friend of the architect Sir John Soane (1753–1837), in whose house in Lincoln's Inn Fields this picture still hangs. The architect had a Shakespeare Recess, a little shrine that vividly encapsulates the early nineteenth-century's preoccupation with the poet. It includes a cast of the figure from the poet's tomb, two paintings on Shakespearean subjects by Henry Howard (1769–1847) and engravings of characters from Shakespeare by John Hamilton Mortimer (1740–79). Soane bought Mrs Pope's picture for £31.10.0, and she provided him with a manuscript list of the flowers. This is preserved in the museum, the flowers listed on one side and the plays in which they appear on the other. Beneath a bust of Shakespeare, loosely derived from that by the French sculptor Louis-François Roubiliac

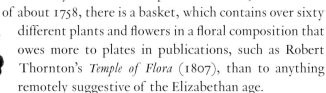

of about 1758, there is a basket, which contains over sixty different plants and flowers in a floral composition that owes more to plates in publications, such as Robert Thornton's *Temple of Flora* (1807), than to anything remotely suggestive of the Elizabethan age.

Opposite & left The Bust of Shakespeare Encircled by All the Flowers Mentioned in his Works, Clara Maria Pope, c. 1835 Watercolour on paper, 85 × 65 cm (33⅜ × 25½ in.)

When daisies pied, and violets blue,
And lady-smocks all silver white,
And cuckoo-buds of yellow hue
Do paint the meadows with delight,
The cuckoo then on every tree,
Mocks married men, for thus sings he:
                    Cuckoo,
Cuckoo, cuckoo O word of fear,
Unpleasing to a married ear.

When shepherds pipe on oaten straws,
And merry larks are ploughmens clocks,
When turtles tread, and rooks and daws,
And maidens bleach their summer smocks,
The cuckoo then on every tree,
Mocks married men, for thus sings he:
                    Cuckoo,
Cuckoo, cuckoo, O word of fear,
Unpleasing to a married ear.

SHAKESPEARE & THE VICTORIAN LANGUAGE OF FLOWERS

I T was inevitable that Shakespeare's symbolic use of flowers would take off in an age that witnessed a profusion of flowers, thousands new to the country. The eighteenth century had been the age of the landscape garden. Flower gardens did exist, but for the most part they were enclosed spaces to be visited away from the main house. The poet-gardener William Mason's famous and innovative informal flower garden at Nuneham Courtenay in Oxfordshire, which had been laid out in 1772, became the acme of fashion and was widely copied. Inspired by the garden in Jean-Jacques Rousseau's *La nouvelle Héloïse* (1769), Nature was to inspire feelings of virtue as well as pleasure. There was a fashionable cult of flowers led by George III and his family in the new royal gardens at Kew and Frogmore in Windsor.

As a consequence, flower painting entered a golden age in the work of Francis Bauer (1758–1840), and botanizing became a pursuit deemed suitable for young ladies. With the arrival of a female monarch, Queen Victoria, in 1837, the floodgates opened to a floral paradise in the form of massive displays of annuals, the formation of exotic plant collections and the proliferation of extravagantly illustrated books. Flowers became the perfect vehicle for what was to become the quintessential age of sentiment, carrying Shakespeare's flowers to their summit.

One aspect of that was a minor revival of the Renaissance emblematic tradition, recast in what we now call the language of flowers. This fashion was set in motion in 1834, three years before Victoria came to the throne, by the translation into English of a book by Louise Cortambert, who wrote

Opposite Concluding song from *Love's Labour's Lost*, Act 5, Scene 2, illuminated by H. C. Hoskyns Abrahall in *Songs of Shakespeare*, 1866

under the pen-name of Charlotte de La Tour, entitled *Le langage des fleurs* (1818). This work gave birth to two great waves of flower-language books running through the Victorian period, the first spate during the 1830s and 1840s and the second through the 1870s. The fashion continued into the twentieth century with a steady flood of books, the most famous of which is that by Walter Crane, *Flowers from Shakespeare's Garden* (1906). With the Romantic movement at its height – set against the poetry of Wordsworth for instance – these books hardly rise above being a simpering stream into which Shakespeare's flowers were inevitably inserted.

Flowers, for the Victorians, took on the role of a moral encyclopaedia, to which the key was one of their numerous flower dictionaries. These, almost without exception, take the form of an alphabetical list of plants and flowers, accompanied by their meaning. *The Language of Flowers: An Alphabet of Floral Emblems*, published in 1857, is a typical example of one of these dictionaries, which all duplicate each other and ascribe the same meaning to the plants and flowers. Here is a tiny section of what appears under the letter D for Daisy:

Daisy, Double	❧	*Participation*
Daisy, Garden	❧	*I share your sentiments*
Daisy, Ox Eye	❧	*A token*
Daisy, Party-coloured	❧	*Beauty*
Daisy, Red	❧	*Unconscious*
Daisy, White	❧	*Innocence*
Daisy, Wild	❧	*I will think of it*

In these books, plants were categorized with such detailed nuances of meaning that a simple posy sent by a lover to his *inamorata* could in fact carry quite an intricate message, which, it was assumed, she would have no difficulty unravelling. Inevitably, when this French fashion crossed the Channel, it called for naturalization. And this was achieved by drawing heavily on the works of the English poets; Shakespeare's contribution found an honoured place early on. Here is how the ninth, 1843, edition of

Opposite Binding and various pages from *Flowers from Shakespeare's Garden*, illustrated by Walter Crane, 1909 edition

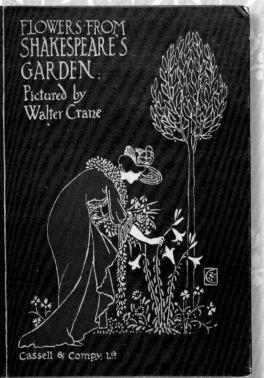

FLOWERS·FROM
SHAKESPEARE'S
GARDEN:
Pictured by
Walter Crane

Cassell & Compy. Ld.

9

lilies of all kinds,

29.

and with
eglantine."

Midsummer Night's
Dream, Act ii., Sc. 1

18.

"Their lips were four red roses on a stalk,
Which in their summer beauty kissed each other"

Richard III., Act iv. Sc. 3

Hark! hark! the lark at heaven's gate sings
And Phœbus 'gins arise.
His steeds to water at those springs
On chalic'd flowers that lies:
And winking Mary-buds begin
To ope their golden eyes:
With everything that pretty bin,
My lady sweet, arise,
Arise, arise.

The Language of Flowers, dedicated to Queen Victoria's mother the Duchess of Kent, expresses it in the introduction:

SHAKESPEARE has evinced in several of his plays a knowledge and a love of flowers, but in no instance has he shewn his taste and judgment in the selection of them with greater effect than in forming the coronal wreath of the lovely maniac, Ophelia. The Queen describes the garland as composed of crow-flowers, nettles, daisies, and long-purples; and there can be no question that Shakespeare intended them all to have an emblematic meaning.

The anonymous author holds this up as 'an exquisite specimen of emblematic or picture-writing'. They are all wild flowers, he or she writes, denoting Ophelia's deranged state, and each flower brings its meaning: the crow-flower 'fair maid', nettles 'stung to the quick', daisies 'her virgin bloom' and long-purples 'under the cold hand of death'.

One of the authors of the second wave of flower books, John Ingram, summed up the whole relationship of Shakespeare to the Victorian cult of flowers when he wrote in *Flora Symbolica; or, the Language and Sentiment of Flowers* (1869): 'Shakespeare tells us "Fairies use flowers for their charactery" and so, he might have added, do mortals.'

The Victorian cult of flowers in this emblematic sense was not to run out of steam until the turn of the century. What it achieved was the acquisition of a wide knowledge of the poet's own flowers, particularly by the female members of the middle and upper classes. Through it real flowers became interlocked in people's minds with those they had read about in his plays and poetry. The cult of flowers was in a sense a trivial aspect of a far wider vision, which was to lead to the creation of Shakespeare's New Place garden.

Opposite The Serenade from *Cymbeline*, Act 2, Scene 3, illuminated by H. C. Hoskyns Abrahall in *Songs of Shakespeare*, 1866

Above Decoration from Grindon's *Shakspere Flora*, 1883

SHAKESPEARE THE GARDENER

I N 1864, thirty years after the translation of *Le langage des fleurs*, came the first book entirely dedicated to Shakespeare's plants and flowers, Sidney Beisley's *Shakespeare's Garden, or the Plants and Flowers Named in his Works Described and Defined*. The book was published in Stratford-upon-Avon by 'The Trustees and Guardians of Shakespeare's Birthplace', and was surprisingly un-illustrated. It remains even today the standard work, and was reissued as late as 2009 in paperback. By the time of its publication John Ruskin (1819–1900) had observed in his *The Poetry of Architecture* (1837–38) that 'we must read Shelley to learn how to use flowers, and Shakespeare to learn to love them'. Taking Shakespeare as the supreme poet of Nature, Beisley was led to conclude that his 'knowledge

of *Botany* was not less than that of any other branch of natural history he investigated and described'. The format that follows is the reverse of that of its numerous successors in the genre, that is, the later publications start with the plant or flower and not, as Beisley does, the plays.

Beisley's book has twenty-six chapters in all, each opening with a listing of all the plants that occur in a particular play with their common as well as proper botanical names. The opening of the chapter on *Love's Labour's Lost* is typical: 'The plants named in this play are *Daisy* (Bellis perennis), *Violet* (Viola odorata), *Lady smocks* (Cardamine pratensis), *Cuckoo buds* (Ranunculus Ficaria).'

Each plant is then elaborated upon with quotations from the play text and fleshed out with descriptions of the plant or flowers, within both its botanical and historical context. The decision to organize by play instead of plant gives a curiously unsatisfactory result.

Of far more significance was the next publication that re-worked this theme: the work of a major plantsman of the era, Canon Henry Nicholson Ellacombe (1822–1916). Henry Ellacombe was an influential and popular garden writer, and his book *The Plant-Lore and Garden-Craft of Shakespeare*, published in 1878, was an expansion of a series of articles, which the author had published the previous year in *The Garden*, the journal of the Royal Horticultural Society. *The Plant-Lore and Garden-Craft of Shakespeare* ran into three editions and reflected Ellacombe's passion for Shakespeare, which was also captured in his second, privately printed, work, *Shakespeare as an Angler* (1883). The contents of the three editions vary, the most significant difference being the addition of illustrations, sixteen plates and sixty-four text figures by Major E. Bengough Ricketts to the 1896 edition published by Edward Arnold. In his memoir of Ellacombe, published in 1910, Sir Arthur Hill gives an account of this book in which he captures its ambience: 'a succinct and readable account of the love which attaches to certain popular favourites, an account which is neither the twitter of the

Opposite & above Binding and title-page decoration of Henry Nicholson Ellacombe's *The Plant-Lore and Garden-Craft of Shakespeare*, 1878

sentimental drawing-room-table flower-book, nor a dry-as-dust compilation intended to illustrate the learning of the compiler.'

What is important about Ellacombe's book is that in it Shakespeare's plants cross over into reality, written about by a man who knew and grew many of them in his own famous garden at Bitton in Gloucestershire. With this book we are within reach of making an actual Shakespeare garden. And here, for the first time, the playwright is claimed as a hands-on gardener:

I. . .propose to claim him as a fellow-labourer. A lover of flowers and gardening myself, I claim Shakespeare as equally a lover of flowers and gardening; and this I propose to prove by showing how, in all his writings, he exhibits his strong love for flowers, and a very fair, though not perhaps a very deep, knowledge of plants.

The format too is different, starting this time with the plants rather than the plays, and arranging the plants alphabetically, like a dictionary, starting with aconitum and ending with yew.

The entry on eglantine is a typical example of Ellacombe's treatment of Shakespeare's flowers. It opens by quoting the famous lines spoken by Oberon from *A Midsummer Night's Dream* (see below) and a less well-known passage from a speech by Arviragus in *Cymbeline*. He then goes on:

IF Shakespeare had only written these two passages they would sufficiently have told of his love for simple flowers. None but a dear lover of such flowers could have written these lines. There can be no doubt that the Eglantine in his time was the Sweet Briar – his notice of the sweet leaf makes this certain.

I know a bank where the wild thyme blows,

Where oxlips and the nodding violet grows,

Quite overcanopied with luscious woodbine,

With sweet musk-roses, and with eglantine.

OBERON, *A MIDSUMMER NIGHT'S DREAM*, ACT 2, SCENE I

‡ 2 *Rosa syl.odora flore duplici.*
The double Eglantine.

3 *Rosa Canina inodora.*
The Brier Rose, or Hep tree.

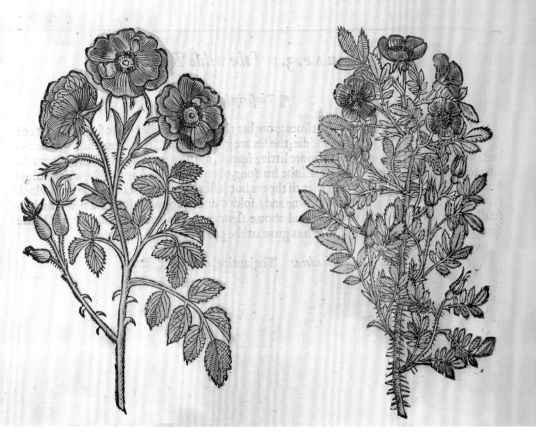

The eglantine and the briar rose from John Gerard's *The Herball*, 1633 edition

He then proceeds to mentions of it by Milton and Herrick and finally turns his attention to the actual plant:

It is a native of Britain, but not very common, being chiefly confined to the South of England. I have found it on Maidenhead Thicket. As a garden plant it is desirable for the extremely delicate scent of its leaves, but the flower is not equal to others of the family.

And Ellacombe rounds off his account of eglantine with a quote from John Gerard's *Herball, or Generall Historie of Plantes* (1597) on the use of its fruit as a rarefied cooking ingredient in 'banqueting dishes'.

Who, when he lived, his breath and beauty se[t]
Gloss on the rose, smell to the violet?

VENUS AND ADONIS, LINES 935–36

Others were to follow the canon's formula until well into the twentieth century. Although they all go over the same material, each has some attitude or preference that colours their presentation of the same material. For Leo H. Grindon in his *Shakspere Flora* (1883), the playwright is

> THE poet, supremely, of Nature. He sees everything, both great and small, which environs us, and this not only with the eye of an artist, intent upon loveliness of form and colour, but with the profounder comprehensiveness which gives ability to interpret, asking what may these things signify, what may be their story for the imagination. He is not slow either to observe the phenomena of which science takes special cognizance.

Twelve years later H. W. Seager, in his *Natural History in Shakespeare's Time* (1896), gathers together 'a collection of the quaint theories about Natural History accepted by Shakespeare and his contemporaries'. It includes the usual alphabetical list running from aconitum to yew as does the Stratford resident and journalist Frederick G. Savage's *The Flora and Folk Lore of Shakespeare* (1923), which began its life as a series of articles in the *Stratford-upon-Avon Herald* between 1909 and 1916. By the time Savage's book was published, the New Place garden had already been made.

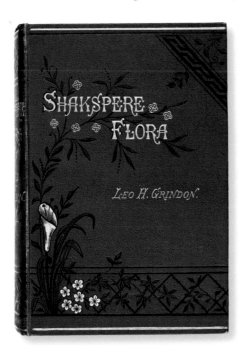

Opposite & left
Illustrations and binding of Leo H. Grindon's *Shakspere Flora*, 1883. Grindon added his own notes to verses by Shakespeare that mentioned trees, plants and flowers.

SHAKESPEARE & GARDEN HISTORY

I N *The Plant-Lore and Garden-Craft of Shakespeare* (1878), its author, Henry Ellacombe, considers the possibility of making an authentic Shakespeare garden, and, in the second part of his book, contemplates Elizabethan gardening for the first time. The canon was steeped in the old gardening books of Tudor and Stuart England, which he had in his vicarage library. Moreover he sets these gardens in a favourable light, saying that today we would have 'no difficulty in realising them both in their general form and arrangement'. This makes Ellacombe the first author to open the door to recreation, although, ultimately, he did not think that it would be desirable to reinstate Elizabethan gardens, as they were far too formal and artificial for contemporary taste. What appealed to Ellacombe about Shakespeare's flowers was that they were 'thoroughly English'. That observation presents us with another reason for the redis-covery of Elizabethan garden style. Ellacombe's eulogy of the Elizabethan knot garden filled with its native blooms came, in fact, at a particular moment in the history of garden style. This was to contribute substan-tially to the realization of an accurate Shakespeare garden.

What attracted Ellacombe to Elizabethan gardening was that it offered ammunition in the battle against mid-Victorian bedding out. The prac-tice of filling flowerbeds for the summer months with tender annuals from Central and South America was the quintessence of High Victorian garden style. This fashion was only to wane in the aftermath of the publications of William Robinson (1838–1935). Wild English flowers were to be his life's enduring passion and his books *The Wild Garden* (1870) and *The English Flower Garden* (1883) came to be the bibles of a garden revolution, which swept away the bedding out of annuals and replaced them with swathes of lawn and simplified borders of native herbaceous plants. Ellacombe is eloquent in his attack on the bedding-out system, which produces 'masses

He hath a garden circummured with brick,

Whose western side is with a vineyard backed;

And to that vineyard is a plankèd gate,

That makes his opening with this bigger key.

This other doth command a little door

Which from the vineyard to the garden leads.

ISABELLA, *MEASURE FOR MEASURE*, ACT 4, SCENE I

Above & overleaf An Elizabethan garden in autumn (above) and summer (overleaf) taken from Crispijn van de Passe's *Hortus Floridus*, 1614. Elizabethan gardens were designed to be beautiful in every season.

of flowers, the individual flowers being of no importance, except so far as each flower contributes its little share of colour to the general mass'. The Elizabethan garden is seen in dramatic contrast as an ally in this patriotic revival of old-fashioned flowers:

> THE beds were planted inside their margins with a great variety of plants, and apparently set as thick as possible. . . These were nearly all hardy perennials, with the addition of a few hardy annuals, and the great object seems to have been to have had something of interest or beauty in these gardens at all times of year. The principle of these old gardeners was that 'Nature abhors a vacuum', and, as far as their gardens went, they did their best to prevent a vacuum occurring at any time.

With this discourse on sixteenth-century gardening, we touch on the final element, which has so far been missing. For an authentic Shakespeare garden to be planted, people had not only to begin to see gardening in terms of a succession of styles but also to appreciate those styles and revive them. From the point of view of that line of thought, this particular tack began under a cloud. There is an irony in the fact that the rise of Shakespeare as a literary divinity under the aegis of Garrick occurred at precisely the moment when the landscape style, formulated by William Kent (1685–1748) and epitomized by the work of 'Capability' Brown (1716–83), reached its apogee. How could anyone brought up to admire the gentle hills, lakes and copses of trees so carefully arranged by 'Capability' Brown and his followers have any interest in an Elizabethan knot garden? This was the era in which the flower garden was banished from the vicinity of the house.

The earliest work that might be described as a history of English gardening is Horace Walpole's *Essay on Gardening* (1771). In this, any form of gardening before William Kent and the landscape style, bar the medieval deer park, is trashed. Indeed he is puzzled as to how it took so long for the English to reach what to him was a style both natural to its peoples and expressive of their political principles. All styles that preceded the landscape one were 'impotent displays of false taste'. These, based on descriptions of the Garden of Eden in Milton's *Paradise Lost* (1667) and on the landscape paintings of Claude Lorrain (1600–82) with their evocation of wood and water, valleys and glades, were the antithesis of the knot gardens of Gloriana's England.

Any revival of earlier garden styles was therefore impossible before the advent of the picturesque, an aesthetic that was first codified in Sir Uvedale Price's *Essay on the Picturesque as Compared with the Sublime and the Beautiful* (1794). The picturesque was never a precise style, for its aim was to create a building and surroundings, a garden and a park, which would form a picture enlivened by variety, movement and asymmetry. Using architecture and gardening as stage scenery, it also introduced buildings in the style of distant countries to the garden, as well as opening a door that allowed voyages across time back into the past. In gardening terms its high priest was to be Humphry Repton (1752–1818) who, in 1814, designed gardens in what he believed to be the Elizabethan manner for a house of that era at Beaudesert in Staffordshire.

The earliest essay in a past historical style was about the Monks' Garden at Ashridge in Hertfordshire for the 7th Earl of Bridgewater, designed to recall the monastery gardens that had once stood on the site. In his Red Book for this garden (1813), Repton wrote frankly of the boredom of the modern pleasure-ground: 'we soon tire of the sameness of the gravel walks, in serpentine lines, with broad margins of grass, and flowers, and shrubs.' Instead he proposes 'to go back to those ancient trim gardens, which formerly delighted the venerable inhabitants of this venerable spot, as appears from the trim box hedges of the monks' garden, and some large yew trees still growing in rows near the site of the monastery'. 'I hope,' he writes, 'there is no more absurdity in collecting gardens of different styles, dates, characters, and dimensions, in the same enclosure, than in placing the works of a Raphael and a Teniers in the same cabinet.' It is hard to guess what his source was for the Monks' Garden, which resembles a row of tombs made into flowerbeds with headstones, but virtually all the gardens at Ashridge signal a return to the formality of the pre-Kent era.

How sweet the moonlight sleeps upon this bank!
Here will we sit, and let the sounds of music
Creep in our ears. Soft stillness and the night
Become the touches of sweet harmony.

LORENZO, *THE MERCHANT OF VENICE*, ACT 5, SCENE I

The designs for Beaudesert in Staffordshire, although never executed, went far beyond anything at Ashridge. They were designed to reflect exactly the date of the house, seat of the Tudor Lords Paget, whose descendants were now the Earls of Uxbridge. Repton's avowed aim was to restore the 'pristine character' of the historic mansion and to ensure accuracy, so he enlisted the aid of another architect, John Shaw, who was a member of the Society of Antiquaries. Repton was proud to have discovered from the labourers who worked on the proposed site that 'in the line of the terrace, and other parts of this artificial and architectural garden, we are restoring the place to what they remember it in the beginning of the last century'. This must surely be the first recorded incident of something approaching garden restoration.

Repton's designs for the formal gardens turn the clock back not, as he thought, to the age of Elizabeth I, but rather to the second half of the seventeenth century, one of them being a box-edged *parterre de broderie* with a fountain at its centre. The *parterre de broderie* was the seventeenth-century successor of the Tudor knot garden. In it box was planted in mirror-image patterns in the swirling baroque manner. The work of Repton's son, John Adey Repton (1775–1860), is even more skewed towards antiquarian revivalism. In the Red Book for Woburn Abbey (1805), a lodge in the guise of a fifteenth-century half-timbered house is given gardens to match, with topiary, a maze and parterres containing 'Rosemary, Columbine, Crowfoot, Clove-Pinks, Marigold, Double-Daisy, Monkshood, Southernwood, Pansies, White Rose, Yellow Lilies, Turk's Cap'.

All of this signals something else that would also pave the way to the New Place garden. In the era of the landscape, flower gardens were banished from proximity to the house and became enclosures to which the visitor walked. This was to be reversed in the Regency period, resulting in flower gardens being planted near the house. As early as 1805 Repton had produced a design 'in the ancient formal style' for a flower garden at White Lodge in Richmond Park for Lord Sidmouth.

Opposite Pink from John Gerard's *The Herball*, 1597

Left Detail from the title page of John Gerard's *The Herball*, 1633

1 *Caryophyllus maximus multiplex.*
The great double Carnation.

he flowers are sweet, their colours fresh and trim

THE QUEST FOR THE PAST

THE first English book to publish garden designs in the geometric style found in Italian Renaissance gardens was *Hints on the Formation of Gardens and Pleasure Grounds* (1812) by John Claudius Loudon (1783–1843). Ten years later, in the first edition of his *Encyclopaedia of Gardening* (1822), Loudon actually wrote a history of gardening in the British Isles, which includes two short paragraphs on gardens during the reigns of Elizabeth I and James I. Elizabethan and Jacobean styles, along with Tudor and Gothic, were mingled together in an unsorted jumble with no clear notion of each being a distinct and separate style. Then, in the 1840s, enough had been published for the Elizabethan and Jacobean garden to take on meaningful substance. The key figure in that revival was the architect C. J. Richardson (1806–71), a pupil of Sir John Soane.

Richardson was to produce a whole series of publications, which would enable those who wished to create the semblance of a garden of the kind Shakespeare might have known to do so. *Observations on the Architecture of England during the Reigns of Queen Elizabeth and King James* (1837) laments the loss of the old gardens and goes on to say that:

> THE most important and interesting feature of the gardens were the terraces, imitated from the Italian, and (where the ground favoured the design) ranged successively one above another, and connected with stone steps and balustrades. . .The rest of the designs for gardens belonging to mansions of this description included parterres, bowers, and perspectives, – fountains, canals, and fish-ponds. A bowling-green formed an essential part of the plan, and not unfrequently a wilderness and labyrinth were included in it.

Opposite A labyrinth, or maze, formed with low hedges was a popular feature in early seventeenth-century gardens.

The forme and shape of Bilboquet, which
is an instrument to take the meafure of rounds, as we
haue declared before.

The forme of a Labyrinth.

The moon shines bright. In such a night as this,
When the sweet wind did gently kiss the trees
And they did make no noise. . .

LORENZO, *THE MERCHANT OF VENICE*, ACT 5, SCENE I

He then proceeds to provide detailed illustrations of the terracing at Claverton, Bath, which was to be so influential that it is still produced to this day by manufacturers of reconstituted-stone garden ornaments.

The result of this was a series of romantic, historicizing gardens, which recreated the age of Shakespeare more through the eyes of Sir Walter Scott's *Kenilworth* (1821) than those of Thomas Hill's *The Gardeners Labyrinth* (1577). These included one by Sir Charles Barry at Gawthorpe in Lancashire, the terraces and maze still at Hatfield House, Hertfordshire, and, in 1847, Edward Bulwer-Lytton's Knebworth in Hertfordshire, laid out by himself 'in the style favoured in the reign of James I with the stone balustrades, straight walks, statues and elaborate parterres'. These were all gardens that accorded with the picturesque principle of prospect, but there were others which also looked back for something very different: the English Renaissance garden as a series of enclosed units of the kind described by Francis Bacon (1561–1626) in his famous essay 'Of Gardens' (see pages 102–7). What was to become the *locus classicus* of the style, Levens Hall, Westmorland, with its quite extraordinary topiary was depicted in the first volume of the hugely influential work by Joseph Nash, *The Mansions of England in the Olden Time* (1839–49). Here recreating the past was taken a stage further: surviving interiors of Elizabethan and Jacobean houses were brought to life by inserting into them figures dressed in correct period costume.

So far old houses had been given gardens in period styles but as revivalism took off, new houses in a variety of period styles began to lay out gardens to match the house. The first contemporary garden to respond to this was Arley Hall, Cheshire, one which, as we shall see, was to be an important source for the New Place garden. R. E. Egerton-Warburton laid out Arley in the 1840s by executing the principle that a garden should reflect the historic architectural style of the house. Its most famous feature was its double borders divided into sections with topiary buttresses.

Opposite above Engraving by J. Browne after a painting by W. Hodges RA, *The Merchant of Venice, Act V, Scene 1*. Belmont: a grove or green place before Portia's house

Opposite below Trellis from Gervase Markham's *The Countrie Farme*, 1616

Detail from *Susannah and the Elders, an Allegory of the Transience of Life*,
Frans Floris the elder, *c.* 1550. Oil on panel, 44 × 57 cm (17½ × 22½ in.)

Ernest Law modelled his design for the tunnel arbour at New Place on the
tunnel featured in this painting.

Neither Shakespeare nor his flowers have figured in any of these revivals so far and, indeed, the so-called Elizabethan and Jacobean gardens were more often than not bedded out in High Victorian style with gaudily coloured annuals in the summer months. Already by the close of the 1840s, these revivalist gardens became the subject of a bitter attack by an influential professor of botany at the University of London, John Lindley (1799–1865). His essay entitled 'On the Arrangement of Gardens and Pleasure Grounds in the Elizabethan Age' was published in the *Journal of the Horticultural Society* for 1848. This is a savage indictment of the attempt to revive the Elizabethan style. Nothing in it is worthy, he writes, of a noble mansion. The arbour as a garden feature is held up to ridicule: 'this idea alone relishes exceedingly of the taste adapted to the comfort of modern tea-gardens.' No style, he believed, could be 'more painful still to a man of true taste'. Knots and other features of the garden enumerated by Francis Bacon in his essay only evoked horror to him, evidence of the 'false fashion of the Elizabethan age', 'no enthusiast. . .in favour of the Elizabethan style in architecture, would seriously press, as an accompaniment to the revival of that style, the resuscitation of the fashion in gardening. The truth is that such a notion involves too many contradictions in taste and absurdities in fact to be tolerated by any rational man.' He winds this tirade up with a final resounding damnation:

To revive Elizabethan gardening as a whole, and in all its principles, would be like reviving the pedantry of the age as well as its learning – its euphuism as well as its pure old prose and splendid poetry – its rude and coarse social customs as well as its chivalrous spirit; and would be in each of these cases as in all, a clear offence against good taste.

Not until thirty years after this onslaught would there be a reaction against High Victorian bedding out, which led to Elizabethan gardening being viewed in a favourable light again. Shakespeare's flowers were to enjoy a return to favour as cottage garden plants whose very existence by the 1860s were seen to be threatened by the plant explosion of the mid-Victorian period. Topiary began to be revived and, by the 1870s and 1880s, a whole series of what became known as old-fashioned gardens were laid out with clipped yew hedges, stately walks, flower-bespangled arbours

Away before me to sweet beds of flowers.
Love-thoughts lie rich when canopied
with bowers.

ORSINO, *TWELFTH NIGHT*, ACT I, SCENE I

Detail from *Anne Hathaway's Cottage*, David Woodlock, *c.* 1900
Watercolour on paper, 35 × 29 cm (13¾ × 11½ in.), showing hollyhocks
and classic cottage-garden planting

and plant-bedecked walls. Flowerbeds were edged with box and filled with 'old-fashioned' flowers, valued for their literary and aesthetic associations by the Pre-Raphaelites among others and by an even more influential figure, William Morris.

Penshurst Place in Kent was an early instance of what was an attempt to turn the clock back more accurately. There, from the 1850s, the architect George Devey (1820–86) returned to a formal garden made up of a series of enclosures. It was to be hugely influential, as it was open to the public. During the 1870s Lady Louisa Egerton laid out just such a garden to complement one of the grandest of Elizabethan houses, Hardwick Hall in Derbyshire, as did Constance, Countess of Lothian, for one of the greatest of Jacobean houses, Blickling Hall in Norfolk. Nor were these old-fashioned gardens just for old houses: one of the most spectacular was created in 1884 around a neo-Jacobean house, Hewell Grange in Worcestershire, inspired by Francis Bacon's famous essay 'Of Gardens'. This key text inspiring garden-making was precisely the one condemned by Lindley: nevertheless, Bacon's essay was referred to again and again by everyone who wrote on gardens in the decades leading to 1914.

It is during this period that we get our first Shakespeare garden. In 1892 London County Council created a new municipal park out of the grounds

Lavender

Mint

of Brockwell Park in Herne Hill, South London. There, in what had been the old walled-kitchen garden, all the flowers and herbs mentioned in the plays were planted in what must have been a well-known and possibly highly influential garden. It was J. J. Sexby, the first officer of the London County Council Parks Department, who introduced it. The result was so successful that Sexby initiated gardens of a similar kind in other London parks. Brockwell Park's accuracy is doubtful, judging from its description by that major pioneer of English garden history Alicia Amherst (1865–1941), who, in her book *A History of Gardening in England* (1906), describes many non-Elizabethan flowers, such as dahlias and calceolarias.

Even more influential, however, must have been the Shakespeare border made by Frances Maynard, Lady Brooke, subsequently Countess of Warwick (1861–1938). Daisy, as she was known, was the mistress of an era, a woman who was seductive, impulsive, dangerous yet generous of heart. During the 1890s she had a long liaison with the future Edward VII, an affair that only foundered in 1895 on her conversion to socialism. Frances Maynard was an heiress in her own right and a passionate gardener throughout her life. In the early 1900s, at her own house, Easton Lodge in Dunmow, Essex, she employed men from the Salvation Army home for drunks to lay out a major garden, designed by Harold Peto (1854–1933)

Illustrations from Walter Crane's *Flowers from Shakespeare's Garden*, 1909 edition

Thyme

Rosemary

with more than a passing debt to that described by Francis Bacon. But the Shakespeare border predates that major expansion and belongs to the 1890s, along with a whole series of other highly romantic areas: the 'Roserie', the 'Border of Sentiment', the 'Garden of Scripture' and the 'Garden of Friendship'. The last included heart-shaped pottery plaques bearing the names of the donors of the plants, including that of the then Prince of Wales.

All of this Maynard commemorated in *An Old English Garden*, a highly indulgent volume in which she takes the reader on a guided tour, fortunately one that is illustrated and includes a photograph of the famous Shakespeare border she describes as her greatest passion. She writes:

> IT represents the work of many a winter's evening spent in hunting for quotations [it is difficult to believe that she made no use of one of the series of books in print dealing with Shakespeare's plants and flowers], and in reducing them, when found, to these label limits – delightful pottery butterflies 'twixt green and brown, on each wing of which is the text.

She filled the border with scented herbs, marigolds, eglantine, musk- and damask roses and other flowers associated with Shakespeare.

To receive an invitation to stay at Easton when the Prince of Wales was a guest was a great social accolade and, as the countess was a lady of fashion, her Shakespeare border was asking to be copied. That was aided by the fact that her socialism brought Walter Crane to Easton; Crane's *Flowers from Shakespeare's Garden*, published in 1906, was dedicated to the countess. On the title page he depicts her kneeling in homage, proffering a bouquet of his flowers to a bust derived from the tomb in Stratford church. Walter Crane was the first artist since 1835 who deliberately set out to depict Shakespeare's flowers in a way that can only be described as whimsical, transforming them into chorus girls in costumes more appropriate to a musical comedy at the Gaiety Theatre.

Red rose

News of Lady Warwick's border was not long in crossing the Atlantic. Alice Morse Earle (1851–1911) was an American advocate of 'old-fashioned gardens' and of the Arts and Crafts movement. She knew of the countess's border but thoroughly disapproved of its ceramic butterflies, which she regarded as disfiguring. She went on, however, in her book *Old Time Gardens* (1916), to describe another such border at Hillside, Albury, New York. Hillside arose between 1908 and 1917 under the direction of the landscape architect Fleming Wyoming. Alice Morse Earle published a picture of the Shakespeare border there in her book and responded to it in exactly the literary aesthetic manner of all exponents of the 'old-fashioned garden': 'There was refreshment of the Spirit as well as the senses in this Shakespeare Border, and it stirred the heart of the poet as no modern garden could.' Mrs Earle's over-the-top positive response stretches over several pages and ends unbelievably as follows:

Rose without prickles

I HAD a happy sense, when walking through this garden, that besides my congenial living companionship, I had the company of some noble Elizabethan ghosts; and I know that if Shakespeare and Jonson and Herrick were to come to Hillside, they would find the garden so familiar to them; they would greet the plants like old friends, they would note how fine grew the Rosemary this year, how sweet were the Lady's-smocks, how fair the Gillyflowers...Above all I seemed to see, walking soberly by my side, breathing in with delight the varied scents of leaf and blossom, that lover and writer of flowers and gardens, Lord Bacon – and not in the guise of Shakespeare either.

And with that passing allusion to those who had begun to argue that Francis Bacon was the author of the plays, she ends.

Damask rose

THE ELIZABETHAN GARDEN REDISCOVERED

WE have Shakespeare flowers being planted in borders but as yet there is no sign of planting them into a garden of the type the playwright would actually have recognized. In fact a serious reappraisal of Elizabethan gardens actually went hand in hand with the rise of the 'old-fashioned garden' from the 1860s onwards. This reassessment began as early as 1864, when an article entitled 'Elizabethan Gardening' in *Frazer's Magazine* (reprinted in the *Gardener's Chronicle* the same year) challenged 'the view that all garden style before 1688 was "simple barbarism"'. The anonymous author proceeded to a consideration of Elizabethan gardening as contrasted with 'the violent hues and vulgar blaze' of bedding out. He referred to the favourite style of a 'Garden of Flowers', citing the reference in *Love's Labour's Lost* to the '*curious-knotted garden*' (Act 1, Scene 1): 'what we ought to imitate . . .is the rich colouring and intermixture of warm and cool tints in a Persian carpet, and not the violent hues and vulgar blaze of the French carpet weaver.'

Elizabethan gardens, the informed author goes on to say, were filled with the soft-coloured flowers of the woodlands and he backs this with references to Edmund Spenser, Ben Jonson, Michael Drayton and other poets. They were year-round gardens as opposed to 'a showy blaze of hot colours for a month or two in the hottest part of the year'. Above all he commends the principles of that era's gardens, the fact that garden and house were geometrically linked, that the beds were filled with a harmony of mixed flowers, that they were gardens for every season and that attention

Opposite William Lawson's *A New Orchard and Garden. Or 'The best way for planting, grafting, and to make any ground good, for a rich orchard. . .all grounded on the principles of art, and precepts of experience, being the labours of forty eight yeares of William Lawson'*, 1648 edition

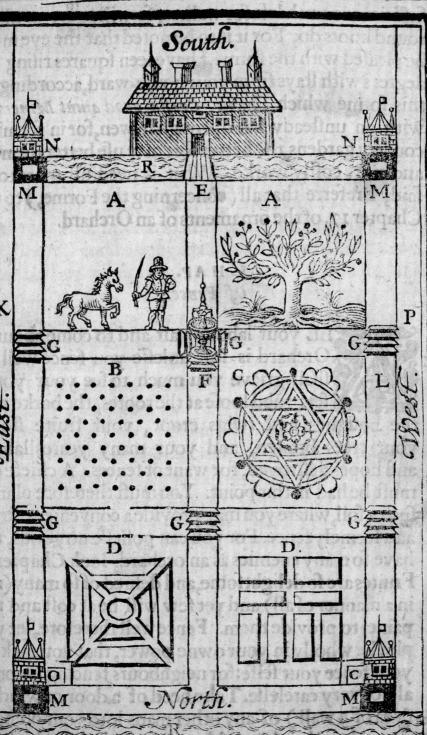

East.

West.

North.

sufficient

A. All these sqare must bee set with trees, the Garden and other ornaments must stand in spaces betwixt the trees, and in the borders and fences

B. Trees 20. yards a sunder.

C. Garden Knots.

D. Kitchen garden

E. Bridge.

F. Conduit.

G. Staires.

H. Walkes set with great wood thicke.

I. Walkes set with great wood round about your Orchard.

K. The out fence.

L. The out fence set with stone fruite.

M. Mount. To force earth for a mount or such like set it round with quick, and lay boughes of trees strangely intermingled tops inward, with the earth in the midle.

N. Still-house.

O. Good standing for Bees, if you have an house.

P. if the river run by your doore and under your mount, it will be pleasant.

was accorded to scent through the planting of sweet herbs. Twelve years later, in 1876, an article entitled 'English Flower Gardens' in *The Garden* went over the same ground: 'Let us see how a garden was regarded at that period of our history when English wits and English taste were confessedly at their brightest and best.'

The last decade of the century and the opening years of the following one was a golden age of garden publishing, enriched by the advent of the half-tone block. The architect J. P. Sedding's *Garden-Craft Old and New* (1891) was a passionately patriotic book vividly reflective of the era in which it was written, when the country was at its imperial zenith. Sedding sets out to glorify an English vernacular style, which he finds firmly rooted in Elizabethan England and Bacon's famous essay. Bacon's garden style is pitted against the landscape one of 'Capability' Brown: 'The first is a garden for a civilised man, the second is a garden for a gipsy.' Two chapters of the book are given over to practicalities and Sedding canonizes for the first time Elizabethan gardening. He boldly writes:

> THE sixteenth century, which saw the English garden formulated, was a time for grand enterprises; indeed, to this period is ascribed the making of England. These gardens, then, are the handiwork of the makers of England, and should bear the marks of heroes.

One year later came an even more important publication, *The Formal Garden in England* (1892) by Sir Reginald Blomfield and F. Inigo Thomas. At the time of publication the book caused something of a sensation, being seen as an attack on the naturalistic style of gardening advocated by William Robinson. The result was a horticultural battle royal of words. Blomfield himself was responsible for a whole series of formal gardens for great houses, ranging from Apethorpe Palace in Northamptonshire to Mellerstain House in Berwickshire. But the book is filled with all the sources needed to plant a true Elizabethan garden, and includes chapters on 'Knots, Parterres, Grass-Work, Mounts, Bowling Greens, Theatres', 'Fish-Ponds, Pleaching, Arbours, Galleries, Hedges, Palisades, Groves' and 'Garden Architecture – Bridges, Gatehouses, Gateways, Gates, Walls, Balustrades, Stairs'. The sixty-seven illustrations draw on Elizabethan and Jacobean books by Thomas Hill (*fl.* 1540s–70s), William Lawson (*fl.* 1570s–1610s) and Gervase Markham (*c.* 1568–1637). And for the first time we have detailed instructions, for instance, as to how precisely a knot garden was planted:

BESIDES the square flower-beds, a more intricate form of bed, designed to fill up a square plot, was much in use. The latter was called a 'knot.' In the sixteenth century it seems to have been usually formed with rosemary, hyssop, and thyme. Five designs for knots are given in *The Gardeners Labyrinth*, which were to be formed entirely of hyssop or thyme. In *The Countrie Housewife's Garden* (1617) Lawson gives 'divers new knots for gardens'. . .All the flowers and herbs for these should, he says be planted by Michaeltide. The borders were to be of 'Roses, thorne, Lavender, rosemaris, isop, sage, or such like,' and filled in with cowslips, primroses, and violets, 'Daffydowndillies,' sweet Sissely, 'go to bed at noone,' and all sweet flowers, and, chief of all, with gilly flowers, the favourite flower of the English Renaissance.

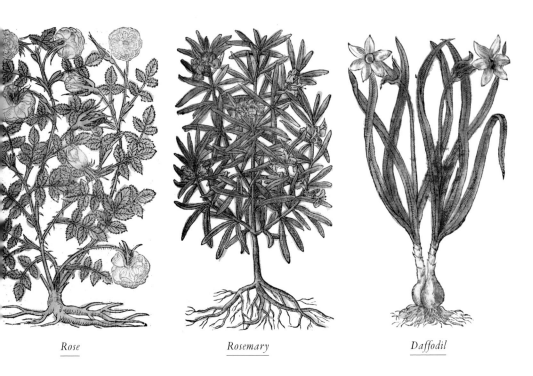

Rose   *Rosemary*   *Daffodil*

Several more pages follow with a focus on knots, and here he reproduces six designs from Gervase Markham's *The Country Housewife's Garden*
(1613). The same detailed treatment is meted out to all the other ingredi-
ents needed to recreate a garden that Shakespeare would have recognized.

Top row Knots from William Lawson's *A New Orchard and Garden*, 1648 edition

Above Knots from Gervase Markham's *The Countrie Farme*, 1616

Below Fruit tree from William Lawson's *A New Orchard and Garden*, 1648 edition

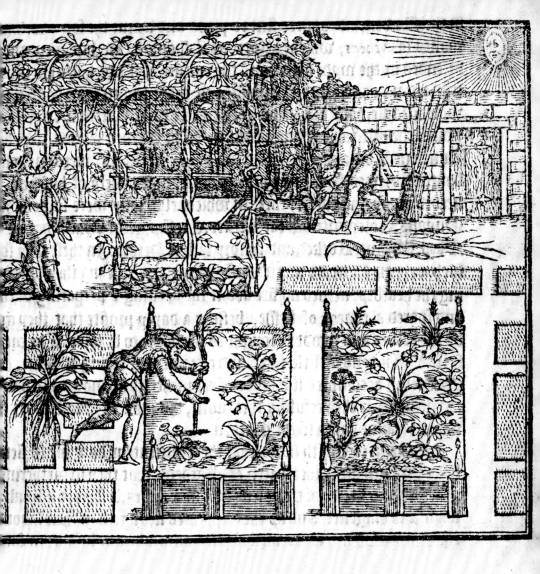

At Christmas I no more desire a rose
Than wish a snow in May's new-fangled shows,
But like of each thing that in season grows.
BIRON, *LOVE'S LABOUR'S LOST*, ACT I, SCENE I

Illustration from the title page of Thomas Hill's *The Gardeners Labyrinth*, 1577, showing gardeners at work in an enclosed garden with raised rectangular beds and an arbour typical of the period

Three years later in 1895, English garden history came of age with Alicia Amherst's *A History of Gardening in England*. No less than three chapters are devoted to Elizabethan and Jacobean gardening: 'Elizabethan Flower Garden', 'Kitchen Gardening under Elizabeth and James I' and 'Elizabethan Garden Literature'. Amherst opens her account of Elizabethan gardening with a eulogy to this great age:

> THE reign of Elizabeth was a golden era in English history, and abounded in men of genius. Among the many branches of art, science, and industry, to which they turned their attention, none profited more from the power of their great minds, than did the Art of Gardening. . .The Elizabethan garden was the outcome of the older fashions in English gardens, combined with the new ideas imported from France, Italy, and Holland. The result was a purely national style, better suited to this country than a slavish imitation of the terraced gardens of Italy, or those of Holland, with their canals and fish-ponds.

Our bodies are our gardens,

IAGO, *OTHELLO*, ACT I, SCENE 3

Left & opposite Illustrations from the title page of John Gerard's *The Herball*, 1597

o the which our wills are gardeners.

Amherst endows the gardens of Shakespeare's England with a kind of imperial aureole, writing as she does eight years on from the Golden Jubilee of Queen Victoria and two years off her Diamond Jubilee. These were the decades when the Elizabethan age was endowed with a heroic aura, which was to cast its spell until well into the twentieth century. Paintings like John Everett Millais's *The Boyhood of Raleigh* (1871), in which an old tar points out to sea and regales the future explorer Walter Raleigh and his friend with tales of new lands to conquer, epitomize the myth. It is mirrored equally in productions like Edward German's opera *Merrie England*, in which great Gloriana herself appears and sings of 'peaceful England', staged in the year of Edward VII's coronation in 1902. And it is also reflected in a golden age of spectacular Shakespeare productions by Sir Herbert Beerbohm Tree (1853–1917) at Her Majesty's Theatre, opened in the year of the Diamond Jubilee.

All the trains of thought and information needed to give us the New Place garden were in place. In the case of Shakespeare and the garden they represent a pile-up of some highly questionable assumptions, starting with the one that Shakespeare was the true mirror of Nature, and therefore his plants and garden lore should be deemed worthy of study and respect. They culminate in the view that, as Shakespeare was our greatest poet living in an age of greatness, it therefore followed that Elizabethan gardening must have been great too.

As a result of all this, a highly successful solicitor, Sir Frank Crisp (1843–1919), made the earliest attempt to recreate accurately an Elizabethan knot garden. Crisp was another pioneer garden historian who was to publish posthumously in two volumes his *Medieval Gardens, 'Flowery Medes' and Other Arrangements of Herbs, Flowers and Shrubs Grown in the Middle Ages, with Some Account of Tudor, Elizabethan and Stuart Gardens* (1924). It appeared too late to affect the planning of the New Place garden, although it is likely that those involved would have seen Crisp's garden at Friar Park near Henley-on-Thames, Oxfordshire, which he began in 1896. He entertained Edward VII and Queen Alexandra regularly in this famous garden during Henley regatta week.

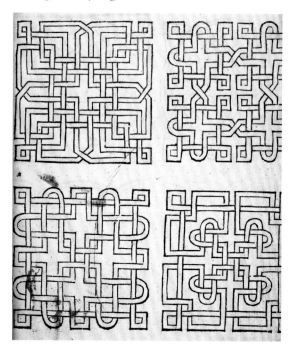

Left & opposite
Illustrations from Thomas Hill's *The Gardeners Labyrinth*, 1577

Knot designs became increasingly elaborate and reflected the interweaving of threads in Elizabethan embroidery and tapestry patterns.

His garden must have been a quite extraordinary creation, including as it did a miniature version of the Matterhorn as a rock garden constructed out of 23,000 tons of rock. The grounds included every type and style of garden, including eight medieval gardens based on those in illuminated manuscripts. It was open every summer for an entry fee, which went to a charity. It included 'sham Swiss mountains and passes, decorated by china chamois. . .and elaborate caves and underground lakes, lit up with electricity, and festooned with artificial grapes, spiders, and other monsters'. Descriptions of this kind hardly inspire confidence in the accuracy of his pioneering recreation of an Elizabethan knot garden. Unfortunately no picture is known. It was based on the woodcuts in Thomas Hill's *The Gardeners Labyrinth* (1577) and on the engravings in Crispijn van de Passe's *Hortus Floridus* (1614). The garden was divided in two, one part a Nosegay Garden, or Garden of Pleasure, and the other a Garden of Herbs of good smell or savour. The flowers were all old-fashioned ones and the herbs totalled some thirty-two in all. Both would have been in the form of knots.

THE NEW PLACE GARDEN & ITS CREATION

NEW Place was purchased by Shakespeare in 1597 and was one of the most substantial properties in Stratford-upon-Avon, indeed the second largest in the town. Contemporary records refer to a 'greate garden', but nothing is known about it; however, the area in which it was situated was large enough to accommodate two barns and an orchard. Shakespeare purchased the property from William Underhill II, who died in 1597. At the close of the fifteenth century the house had belonged to the Clopton family, passing in 1563 to William Bott who, in turn, sold it in 1567 to William Underhill I, a successful lawyer. Placed into that context the playwright would have purchased something that already had a garden in some form.

After the playwright's death, the property passed to his daughter Susanna Hall and then his granddaughter Elizabeth. On her death the

New Place, Stratford upon Avon.

house passed back to the Clopton family again, who, in 1702, altered or rebuilt it. By 1756 it had passed into the hands of the Reverend Francis Gastrell who, in that year, infuriated by 'pilgrims' asking to see the mulberry tree, chopped it down and sold the wood, which was made into Shakespeare souvenirs. Three years later, after a series of altercations with the town's authorities, he deliberately went on to demolish the house itself. In 1876 the site, together with Thomas Nash's house next door, was acquired by the Shakespeare Birthplace Trust.

Shakespeare's Birthplace in Henley Street had already been purchased in 1847. Both properties have a garden history. Indeed what was discussed and carried out at the Birthplace was to be the forerunner for what was to happen at New Place. The earliest reference at the Birthplace to the garden came at the annual trustees' meeting in 1861, when a Mr W. O. Hunt produced a design for laying out the garden and orchard. In July of that year a George Jabet of Birmingham produced a scheme for transforming what was called the Fairy Lawn 'into a Geometrical or Knotted Garden'. So some form of knot garden was on the agenda in the 1860s, but as the gardens disappeared from the agenda we have no way of knowing what was done. All we have are desultory references to various people who, in April 1862, had presented plants to the garden: 'a choice collection of rose trees', 'a variety of shrubs' and, more interestingly, 'a scion of the celebrated mulberry tree planted by Shakespeare'.

The Birthplace garden is small compared with the large area given over to garden at New Place, which was laid out with American pines, horse chestnuts and aucubas, winding paths, stucco vases and lawns dotted with beds filled with annuals during the summer months. That scheme must have been carried out during the winter of 1870 to 1871, for the trustees' minutes record the committee's pleasure in May at 'the great additions and improvements':

THE Gardens have been judiciously laid out, and planted with the choicest trees and shrubs, many of which have been given by inhabitants of the town, and visitors who were desirous of planting them upon this interesting spot.

Opposite A print showing New Place with the Guild Chapel to its left, 1861

In 1878 the New Place gardens were opened to the public. The creator and chronicler of the New Place garden, Ernest Law, writes of this recording his dismay. He was addicted to 'old-fashioned flowers', and therefore considered these additions a horticultural aberration on a site that was a national shrine. He ends his account with a final swipe: 'the whole enclosed with a costly, elaborate and very ugly railing of the finest cast iron!' In his book on the subject, he includes pictures of the garden before his restoration swept it away.

That decision was taken in 1919 under the aegis of the chairmanship of the great Shakespearean authority Sir Sidney Lee (1859–1926), and coincides exactly with the arrival of Ernest Law, the official historian of Hampton Court Palace, as a life-trustee in the May of that year. Law's prolific writings included three books on Shakespearean subjects: *Shakespeare as a Groom of the Chamber* (1910), *Supposed Shakespeare Forgeries* (1911) and *More about Shakespeare Forgeries* (1913).

New Place Gardens, Stratford-on-Avon

Above Postcard of the foundations of New Place garden with
the Guild Chapel to the left, *c.* 1901

Below The Birthplace garden, 1911. It was smaller than the area given to
Ernest Law's New Place garden.

In the summer of 1919 the question of whether to create a bowling green there came up at a trustees' meeting, and then at the 6 November meeting letters were read from Sir Sidney Lee and Lionel Cust, Surveyor of the King's Pictures and a former director of the National Portrait Gallery, and 'various suggestions were discussed for the improvement of the gardens at New Place'. The decision to re-lay it out must have been taken, since in January 1920 Law, who was to be the driving force and designer of the gardens, reported progress on the work and on the plants promised from both Kew Gardens and Hampton Court. The provisional estimate for the new garden was about £500. In March gifts of plants from a number of donors, including Queen Alexandra, the Earl of Pembroke and Lady Fairfax-Lucy of Charlecote Park, Warwickshire, were reported, as well as the gift of £50 from Marie Corelli. Work by then must have been in its final stages, because on 8 April it was decided that a reception was to be held on Shakespeare's birthday, 23 April, to mark the reopening of the garden and also the planting of the royal rose trees. Apart from a few additions in 1922 the garden vanishes thereafter from the official proceedings.

More about all of this can be garnered from the committee's official published Annual Reports, which provide a more sustained account of the making of the new garden. The report for the year ending 31 March 1920 records that it had been busy about the garden with a view to restoring its

The Bowling Green (New Place garden), C. F. Green, 1844
Watercolour on paper, 34 × 57 cm (13⅜ × 22½ in.)
Gentlemen can be seen playing bowls and drinking on
the bowling green with the Theatre Building and the
Guild Chapel in the background.

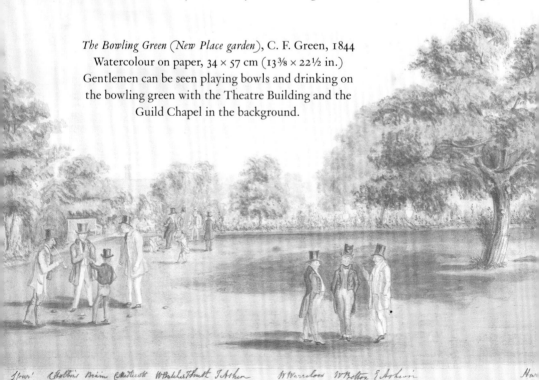

Elizabethan features and that a knot garden had been laid out 'in accord-
ance with authentic contemporary plans' under the direction of Ernest
Law. At the close of 1922 the committee notes with satisfaction that the
creation of the garden 'has drawn to New Place a larger number of visitors
than in any previous year'.

We are fortunate in having an extremely detailed account of this
'restoration', for Law published a fully illustrated one in 1922 entitled
Shakespeare's Garden, Stratford-upon-Avon. There are photographs of the
garden before restoration, the garden in the making, finished and fully
in flower as well as an artist's impression of it peopled by characters in
Elizabethan dress. There were three sections in the New Place garden,
the largest being a lawn acting as a foil to what was designated the 'Long
Border', 'treated', Law writes, 'in the formal fashion of the olden time
. . .being divided into compartments separated by "buttresses" of yew,
supporting "pillars" or columns surmounted by balls'. Into this was
crammed an overflowing herbaceous border of the type advocated by
exponents of 'the old-fashioned garden' – an array of summer and autumn
flowers, including hollyhocks, crown imperials, larkspur, lupins and lilies.
We probably cannot blame Law for that, but rather the lady who actually
carried out the planting. For this Law records the debt owed 'to the energy
and taste of Mrs Flower – wife of Mr A. D. Flower, seven times Mayor of

C F Green Delin 1844

W Stiles   Cooper George J Ward E Slaghton Barron J Cary   J Palmer   Rose   Boot

Stratford-upon-Avon – who arranged and planted them amid all the difficulties of uncertain weather, hurried preparation and very little time, so as to be ready for the formal opening in the spring of 1920'. Does one sense here a touch of Riseholme and Queen Lucia? I think so.

If Law's vision of the long border seems vaguely familiar, it is hardly surprising, for its source was not Elizabethan at all but an early Victorian Elizabethan revival. The arrangement of the border divided up by buttresses of clipped yew is practically lifted directly from those at Arley Hall planted in the 1840s.

At the eastern or lower end of the garden, Law created his second feature: 'A wild bank or heath as Bacon advised.' This recreation of the 'heath or desert' described by the essayist took the form of an irregular bank upon which was planted most of the flowers and herbs mentioned in the poet's writings, 'and where, it is hoped, every species known in his time will eventually find a place'.

But by far the most important and revolutionary part of the scheme was the knot garden and its enclosing raised tunnel arbour: for here Shakespeare's flowers, for the very first time, really did meet a garden structure he would have recognized. The wooden tunnel arbour, a device to provide shelter and shade, was a feature of the medieval garden. Instances can be seen in the illuminations in the fifteenth-century *Très riches heures* of Jean, Duc de Berry. Assimilated into the Renaissance garden, they provided a frame into which was set a new garden form, the knot. That had made its first appearance in engravings in Francesco Colonna's *Hypnerotomachia Poliphili*, published in Venice in 1499. Knots were already in the royal gardens in the 1530s but in the case of England, the earliest designs appear in Thomas Hill's *The Profitable Art of Gardening* (1568) and *The Gardeners Labyrinth* (1577), published under the pseudonym Didymus Mountain.

Ernest Law's border in the New Place garden, 1920s

Law tells us precisely what sources he used to recreate a knot at New Place. Here is what he writes:

> THE enclosing palisade – a very favourite device of Jacobean gardeners – of Warwickshire oak, cleft, is exactly copied from the one in the beautiful tapestry of the 'Seven Deadly Sins' at Hampton Court. . .Next to be noticed is the dwarf wall, of old fashioned bricks – hand-made, sun-dried, sand-finished, with occasional 'flarers,' laid in the Tudor bond, of alternate headers and stretchers with wide mortar joints – is based on similar ones, still extant, of the period. The balustrade of Warwickshire elm is identical, in its smallest detail, with one figured in *The Gardeners Labyrinth*, a book Shakespeare must have consulted when laying out his own Knott Garden. The paths are paved with old stone from Wilmcote, the home of Shakespeare's mother.

So Law firmly sees that local wood and stone are utilized in this new garden. He then tells the reader the source of the four-knot designs:

> THE intricate, interlacing patterns of the Knott beds. . .are taken from Mountaine's book; two from Gervase Markham's 'Country Housewife's Garden' (1613) and one from William Lawson's 'New Orchard and Garden' (1618); and they are composed, as enjoined by those authorities, of box, thrift, lavender-cotton, thyme, and other herbs, with their interspaces filled in with flowers. The old designs have, indeed, been followed with a fidelity and completeness unattempted for 280 years.

In that statement Law was undoubtedly right. And each one of the sources he mentions can be checked to confirm that his knot garden was a quite extraordinary attempt to bring to life the garden that we see in the crude woodcut in *The Gardeners Labyrinth*. But Law has replaced the four raised beds with four knots, each taken from impeccable contemporary sources. An artist's realization of this restored garden for the *Illustrated London News* includes one feature that never came, a central fountain, and the beds were, of course, horrendously overplanted when set side by side with those in the well-known engravings in the *Hortus Floridus* of 1614, where they are correctly spaced wide apart (see pages 49–51).

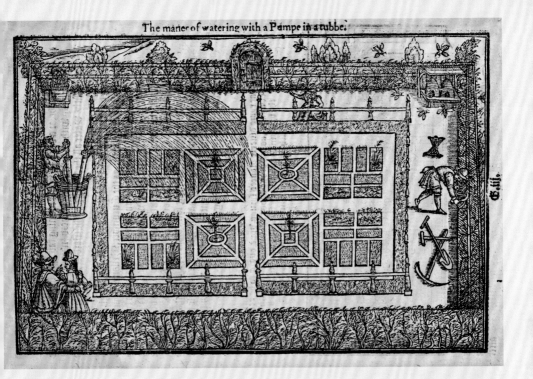

Top Illustration from Hill's *The Gardeners Labyrinth*, 1577, showing how to water using a hand pump. Note the couple on the left having a furtive conversation.

Above An artist's impression from the *Illustrated London News* of the newly restored New Place knot garden with Elizabethan characters at work, as seen in Ernest Law's *Shakespeare's Garden*, 1922.

From a drawing by Mr. A. Forestier, by kind permission of the "Illustrated London News."

THE LONG BORDER AS IT WILL BE. (*See pp.* 20 *and* 21.)

Frontispiece

Above & opposite Frontispiece showing the long border and knot designs from Ernest Law's *Shakespeare's Garden*, 1922

That should not detract from the fact that this recreated Elizabethan garden is not just sentimental curiosity but a milestone in the emergence of garden history and recreation. The worship of Shakespeare as the poet of Nature, the Victorian cult of flowers, the revival of Elizabethan garden styles and the cult of old-fashioned flowers were the interconnecting bypaths which resulted in the first major public attempt in England to accurately recreate a garden of another age. It is a phenomenon, however, that must be placed within a broader perspective. In France the restoration of the great châteaux gardens, such as Vaux-le-Vicomte and Courances, was already underway in the 1870s under the aegis of Henri and Achille Duchêne. Villandry was laid out between 1906 and 1924 as a vast garden in the manner of the French Renaissance, based on those recorded in sixteenth-century engravings. In 1926 the huge garden recreation schemes in Virginia at Colonial Williamsburg began. Law himself was, in 1922, to go on and lay out a second knot, this time at Hampton Court, which still exists.

The New Place knot has one other context. It was laid out two years after a four-year-long world war that had devastated a nation. Here, in the town which had become the shrine of that icon of national achievement and identity, William Shakespeare, a garden was unveiled – a symbol of peace. It was, however, a garden that looked back and not forward. The struggle to raise the money and its modesty speaks of post-war austerity. Amid the turbulence of that era, security and tranquillity were seen to reside in recreating the past.

AFTERMATH: SHAKESPEARE GARDENS
AROUND THE GLOBE

THE story does not end there. Surprisingly the New Place garden had more successors around the globe than in England, both in Europe but more particularly in America. Wikipedia lists no fewer than thirty gardens that claim to be Shakespearean, almost all of them in the United States. Few amount to more than a collection of some of the plants mentioned in the plays and most are little more than an Olde Worlde garden with a sundial at its centre, in the manner of Lucia's.

In the decades between the wars, knowledge of Elizabethan gardens advanced and one book in particular must have been hugely influential, Eleanour Sinclair Rohde's *Shakespeare's Wild Flowers. Fairy Lore, Gardens, Herbs, Gatherers and Bee Lore* (1935), to accord the book its full title. Rohde (1881–1950), who began her career as secretary to Lord Curzon, was a pioneer garden historian, producing a steady stream of books covering such subjects as plants mentioned in the Bible as well as a pioneering study of Tudor and Stuart gardening literature. The Shakespeare garden she presents is modelled on a plan for a small garden in Thomas Hill's *Most briefe and pleasaunte treatise* (1563), the earliest book on gardening printed in the English language.

O, what pity is it That he had not so trimme

GARDENER, *RICHARD II*, ACT 3, SCENE 4

Thomas Hill's *The Gardeners Labyrinth*, 1577, was a bestseller in its time.
Its illustrations still provide valuable detail about how to recreate a small
Elizabethan garden.

d dreſſed hiſ land   As we thiſ garden!

Rohde begins as follows:

T̲HIS garden might be enclosed in various ways – either a hedge
of sweetbriar – Titania's eglantine. . .Or the garden could be
surrounded with wattle fencing against which Ophelia's rosemary
'for remembrance' could be trained. . .The general design of the
garden – i.e., all the beds – could be planted with thick edgings of
lavender, winter savory, rue, thyme, and hyssop. . .The centre of
the garden. . .could be made a knot garden with hyssop and rue. . .
Or if a simpler knot is preferred and made with low-growing herb,
it might be laid out in thyme.

She then goes on to suggest the planting at considerable length,
running through much of the repertory we have encountered already in
the books devoted to the playwright's plants and flowers. She ends by
suggesting that 'At the end of the central path, there might be a simple
arbour "where honeysuckle ripened by the sun forbids the sun to enter."
And at the other end a sundial.'

There is no evidence that anyone actually planted this garden and the
only return to this topic in England is in what was called a Shakespeare
border planted at Charlecote Park in 1973. Charlecote Park was the seat
of the Lucy family, and legend has it that Shakespeare poached deer in the
park. It is now a National Trust property much visited by tourists from

neighbouring Stratford-upon-Avon. The long border
runs north–south and is filled with the trees, shrubs,
flowers and herbs you would expect – trees such as
crab apple, quince and medlar, roses such as *Damascus
Versicolor*, *Gallica Officinalis* and *Centifolia*, flowers like
bluebells and foxgloves and herbs that include the
inevitable rosemary. The design, in the manner of
a Jekyll-esque border, demonstrates that the playwright's plants are little suited to garden design in
the Arts and Crafts style.

The only Shakespeare garden on the European
mainland was laid out in Paris after the Second
World War. That Shakespeare garden goes back to
an incident in the late nineteenth century when a

White mulberry

Scotsman had presented the city with a statue of the poet. This, in 1942, had been removed under the Third Reich and presumably destroyed. After the war there were moves in England to replace the statue, but then came the suggestion of a Shakespeare garden. In 1952 Robert Joffet, then head of Parks and Gardens of the Ville de Paris, alighted upon an abandoned open-air theatre at the Pré Catelan in the Bois de Boulogne. Around this theatre, which was restored, he created a meandering walkway that took the visitor through settings evocative of five plays, which Joffet chose as being realizable in garden terms and making use of the plants and flowers Shakespeare mentions.

The winding route that encircles the theatre begins with the oaks, holly and hawthorn of *As You Like It*'s Forest of Arden. The terrain then ascends upwards towards the blasted heath of *Macbeth*, replete with magnificently sombre yews and mauve and pink heathers, and on into the woodland of *A Midsummer Night's Dream* with a weeping mulberry. Then the path leads downwards once again to a brook with a cascade descending to a flower-fringed pool fit for Ophelia to meet her end in *Hamlet*. Over the stream a willow projects athwart. The finale is Prospero's magic island in *The Tempest*, filled with sun-loving Mediterranean plants, and so back to the beginning and Arden. The garden, which covers one and half acres, opened in 1953 and after a period of neglect was restored in the 1980s, by which time rhododendrons and other thoroughly non-Shakespearean plants had been included, which by then were seen by the French as true to *le style anglais*.

No other country, however, was to become so obsessed with Shakespeare gardens as North America. One of the earliest was that created at the Van

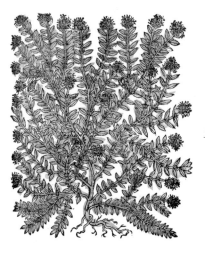

Wild thyme

Wild rosemary

Cortlandt House, Van Cortlandt Park, New York by the Colonial Dames of the State of New York. Van Cortlandt Park is one of the city's biggest, running to over a thousand heavily wooded acres, in the midst of which sits the Van Cortlandt Mansion, a colonial farmhouse built in 1748, which is now a museum run by the Colonial Dames. Two indifferent pictures of this Shakespeare garden appear in *The Shakespeare Garden* (1922) by Esther Singleton (1865–1930). 'Of recent years,' she writes,

> IT has been a fad among American garden lovers to set aside a little space for a 'Shakespeare garden' where a few old-fashioned English flowers are planted in beds of somewhat formal arrangement. These gardens are not, however, by any means replicas of the simple garden of Shakespeare's time, or of the stately garden as worked out by the skilful Elizabethans.

Nonetheless she expresses the hope that her book 'will help those who desire a perfect Shakespeare garden'. Singleton reproduces pictures of the recreated garden at New Place and goes on to list and describe all the plants and flowers referred to in the plays. She discusses gardens in the Elizabethan age, reproducing an abundance of contemporary woodcuts and engravings from the era, as well as gardens Shakespeare would never

The cover picture on Esther Singleton's *The Shakespeare Garden*, 1922, is based on engravings in Crispijn van de Passe's *Hortus Floridus*, 1614 (see pages 49–51).

have remotely recognized. She runs through the whole gamut of mount and knot, sundial and terrace, pleached alley and fountain, and includes a feature utterly unknown to the Tudors, the rock garden.

Oddly, although she reproduces pictures of the Shakespeare garden at Van Cortlandt House, she never refers to it in the text. In the photographs, we see a formal vista across grass flanked by box-edged borders to a bust of Shakespeare on a brick plinth framed by a symmetrical arrangement of trees. The bust is derived from that sculpted by Roubiliac in about 1758. Although a tribute to the poet and doubtless planted with trees, shrubs and flowers of his age, beyond a passing formality there is no attempt here to recreate anything remotely like an authentic Elizabethan garden. Singleton's preoccupation with gardens of that era had another missionary side for much, she believed, was to be learnt from them. 'Today we try for masses of color', whereas 'they blended their hues and even shaded colors from dark to light.' In addition they 'were fastidious about perfume values – something we do not think about to-day'.

Illustration from the title page of Esther Singleton's *The Shakespeare Garden*, 1922

SHAKESPEARE GARDEN, VAN CORTLANDT HOUSE, VAN CORTLANDT PARK, COLONIAL
DAMES OF THE STATE OF NEW YORK

SHAKESPEARE GARDEN, VAN CORTLANDT HOUSE, VAN CORTLANDT PARK, COLONIAL
DAMES OF THE STATE OF NEW YORK

This page from Singleton's book
shows that the Shakespeare garden at
Van Cortlandt House was far from an
authentic Elizabethan garden.

Wild pine tree

Low wild pine tree

This garden was not the only one. Two others were planted in the United States at about the same time. One is in the Brooklyn Botanic Gardens and the other in Golden Gate Park, San Francisco. The latter was planted in the same year as Singleton's book and was conceived as a collection of the many plants mentioned in the author's writings. In recent years it has been re-landscaped and accorded a new formal entrance leading to a new brick path flanked by rows of flowering crab apples. The flower borders contain modern varieties of plants referred to by Shakespeare and modern English roses. There is no attempt here at recreating an Elizabethan style of garden, nor is there at Brooklyn.

That second garden was the result of a benefaction by Henry C. Folger, the founder of the Folger Shakespeare Library in Washington, DC. In 1925 he gave $500 for 'a small Shakespeare Garden' for children. Folger actually stated what his reason for doing so was: 'The important thing is to keep before young people the name of Shakespeare and the fact that he had a decided interest in flowers and plants.' Originally located in the south field of the Children's Garden, it comprised of a collection of trees, shrubs, flowers and herbs mentioned in the plays flanking a limestone path with a wooden bench providing a resting place. Over years the surrounding Austrian pines grew so much that, in 1977, the garden had to be moved to a new site, opening to the public in June two years later. The new location is north of the Fragrance Garden and consists of a sloping semi-circular enclosure held in by a curving brick wall with a comfortable teak bench and a tiered fountain asymmetrically placed in a border. Into this irregular enclosure are gathered some eighty of the plants Shakespeare mentions, each carefully labelled and bearing references to the relevant quotation from the poet's works. The aim was to 'help create the atmosphere of an English cottage garden of the Elizabethan times'.

The obsession with a Shakespeare garden did not end there, for one was incorporated into the International Flower Show held in New York in 1932. This garden had a knot laid out chiefly with Shakespeare's 'flowers of winter'. Moving forwards in time to 1989, the Folger Shakespeare Library re-laid out its garden, this time sited on its east side.

Crab apples

'It is not', runs the official description, 'a scholarly recreation of an authentic Elizabethan garden but an adaptation of features found in Elizabethan gardens with consideration given to the functional use of the garden and to the practicalities of maintenance and funding.' The area is framed by four existing non-Shakespearean magnolia trees and in the middle is a raised approximation to a knot of boxwood, germander and rosemary in-filled with lavender, saffron crocus, thyme, chamomile and clove pink. There is grass and a gravel walkway, serpentine hedges of box, an arbour of white roses, a sundial and a containing hedge of holly. The surrounding beds are planted with daffodils imported from Wales, Christmas roses and ivy.

Over on the West Coast of America a Shakespeare garden was created at the Huntington Library, California. This was first laid out in 1959; it is a spectacular floral display adorning what is described as 'a pastoral woodland glade'. A bust of the playwright is surrounded by a bower of roses from the earliest varieties down to the William Shakespeare rose of the year 2000. There is space too for a host of plants mentioned in his works:

FROM *Hamlet*, there are pansies, fennel, a willow tree, and rosemary; from *Romeo and Juliet*, a pomegranate tree, from *A Midsummer Night's Dream*, violets and thyme; from *The Winter's Tale*, daffodils and maidenheads; and, of course, daisies from *Love's Labour's Lost*.

In a sense this takes us all the way back to where we began.

With that there let it rest and let Ernest Law have the last word on the garden he made on the site of New Place:

F LOWERS then – Shakespeare's flowers – growing in his own garden may serve as symbols and tokens of his countrymen's everlasting affection and reverence – symbols – tokens not less apt nor less perpetual than any monument of stone or brass.

Shakespeare I am sure would have been surprised to have found himself indirectly one of the founding fathers of garden history and restoration, and E. F. Benson mortified that behind Lucia's cultural affectation lay a real seriousness of intent, for which we can now only be grateful. The irony behind this extraordinary story is that we actually have no idea whether Shakespeare ever made a garden at New Place. For all we know he could have lived with the one that he inherited when he bought the property. But the fact that there was a 'greate garden' inevitably triggered a speculation as to what it might have been like. Law's garden stands as a monument to how those at a particular moment in time conceived it. The result is a garden that belongs less to the Elizabethan age than to the era of Edward German's *Merrie England*.

The Huntington Shakespeare garden in California features flowers that were cultivated in England during Shakespeare's lifetime.

INTRODUCTION TO FRANCIS BACON'S ESSAY 'OF GARDENS'

FRANCIS Bacon's famous and oft-reprinted essay 'Of Gardens' first appeared in the 1625 edition of his *Essays*, a year before his death. It, and its companion essay 'Of Building', are both concerned only with ones deemed 'princely', in the case of gardens being not less than thirty acres in extent. This famous essay, with one of the most oft-quoted opening lines in the history of English literature – 'GOD *Almighty* first Planted a *Garden*' – appeared almost a decade on from Shakespeare's death. Bacon himself had an obsession with gardens, not that his own matched what he describes here. Indeed, it sometimes contradicted his dictums. His most famous creation, the water gardens at Gorhambury, his seat in Hertfordshire, flies in the face of his advice that 'pools mar all, and make the garden unwholesome, and full of flies and frogs'. And then there is his withering condemnation of knot gardens – 'you may see as good sights many times in tarts' – reflecting a snobbery about a garden element that had, by that date, become middle class. The same attitude is reflected in his dismissal of topiary: 'images cut out in Juniper, or other garden stuff, they be for children'. What he scorns is exactly the type of garden style that would have been found at New Place.

Bacon's eye is turned towards the only two great palace gardens that he knew well, Lord Burghley's Theobalds in Hertfordshire, which became a royal palace under James I, and the Earl of Suffolk's Audley End in Essex. Both were huge houses with a succession not only of courtyards but of gardens, reflecting Bacon's tripartite division of a princely garden into a 'greene', a 'maine garden' and a 'heath' or wild garden. The 'greene' made up the approach to the house 'because nothing is more pleasant to the eye than green grass kept finely shorn'. In this we touch early on the English obsession with lawns as an essential part of any garden scheme.

Pages from Francis Bacon's 'Of Gardens', 1680 edition

The 'maine garden' is to be square, framed on two sides by tunnel arbours, a Renaissance restyling of a feature of the medieval garden that afforded a place in which to stroll with protection from the sun. In the middle there was to be a circular mount not less than thirty feet high, crowned with a banqueting house. Finally there was the 'heath', 'framed as much as may be to a natural wildness'. And it is to this part of the garden that Bacon gives his heart with his eulogy to 'natural wildness'. It is an area in which his love of scent and his concern with creating a *ver perpetuum*, or perpetual spring, with plants 'for all months in the year', finds fulfilment.

The following essay is taken from *The essays or counsels, civil and moral, of Sir Francis Bacon, Lord Verulam, Viscount St Alban* (1680) owned by the Shakespeare Birthplace Trust.

The original language and spellings have been maintained; however, the modern equivalents of the more obscure words can be found in brackets.

OF GARDENS

by Francis Bacon, 1625

GOD ALMIGHTY first planted a garden; and, indeed it is the purest of human pleasures. It is the greatest refreshment to the spirits of man; without which buildings and palaces are but gross handy-works. And a man shall ever see, that when ages grow to civility and elegancy, men come to build stately, sooner than to garden finely: as if gardening were the greater perfection. I do hold it in the royal ordering of Gardens, there ought to be Gardens for all the months in the year, in which, severally, things of beauty may be then in season. For December and January, and the latter part of November, you must take such things as are green all winter; Holly, Ivy, Bays, Juniper, Cypress trees, Eughs [Yews], Pine-apple trees; Fir-trees, Rosemary, Lavender; Perriwinckle, the white, the purple, and the blew [blue], Germander, Flags, Orenge-trees, Lemmon-trees, and Myrtle, if they be stoved, and Sweet Marjoram warm sets. There followeth for the latter part of January and February, the Mezerion [*Daphne mezereum*] Tree, which then blossoms, Crocus Vernus, both the yellow and the grey, Prim-roses, Anemones, the early Tulippa, the Hyacinthus Orientalis, Chamairis, Fretellaria. For March there comes Violets, specially the single blew, which are earliest, the yellow Daffadil, the Daizy, the Almond-tree in blossom, the Peach tree in blossom, the Cornelian-tree in blossom, Sweet-Briar. In April follow the double White Violet, the Wall-flower, the Stock Gilly-flower, the Couslip [cowslip], Flower-de-Lices, and Lillies of all natures, Rosemary-flower, the Tulippa, the double Piony, the pale Daffadil, the French Hony-suckle, the Cherry-tree in blossom, the Damascen and Plum-trees in blossom, the White Thorn in leaf, the Lelack-tree [lilac tree]. In May and June come Pinks of all sorts, specially the Blush-Pink, Roses of all kinds, except the Musk, which comes later. Hony-suckles, Strawberries, Bugloss [a borage], Columbine, the French Mary gold, Flos Africanus [type of marigold], Cherry-tree in fruit, Ribes, Figs in fruit, Rasps, Vine-flowers, Lavender in flowers, the sweet-Satyrian [type of orchid], with the white flower, Herba Muscaria, Lilium Convallium [lily of the valley], the Apple-tree in blossom. In July come Gilly-flowers of all varieties, Musk-Roses and the Lime-tree in blossom, early Pears and Plums in fruit, Ginnitings, Quadlings [codlings]. In August come Plums of all sorts in fruit, Pears, Apricocks, Barberies, Filbeards [filberts], Musk-Melons, Monks-hoods of all colours. In September comes Grapes, Apples, Poppies of all colours, Peaches, Melo-cotones [type of nectarine],

Double African marigold

Nectarines, Cornelians, Wardens, Quinces. In October, and the beginning of November, come Services, Medlars, Bullises [bullaces, damson-like plums]; Roses cut or removed to come late, Hollyoaks, and such like. These particulars are for the climate of London: but my meaning is perceived, that you may have ver perpetuum, as the place affords.

And because the breath of flowers is far sweeter in the air (where it comes and goes, like the warbling of musick) than in the hand, therefore nothing is more fit for that delight, than to know what be the flowers and plants that do best perfume the air. Roses damask and red are flowers tenacious of their smells, so that you may walk by a whole row of them, and find nothing of their sweetness; yea, though it be in a morning dew. Bays likewise yield no smell as they grow, Rosemary little, nor Sweet-Marjoram. That which above all others yields the sweetest smell in the air, is the Violet, specially the white double Violet, which comes twice a year, about the middle of April, and about Bartholomew-tide. Next to that is the Musk-Rose, then the Strawberry leaves dying with a most excellent cordial smell. Then the flower of the Vines, it is a little dust, like the dust of a Bent, which grows upon the cluster in the first coming forth. Then Sweet-Briar, then Wall-flowers, which are very delightful to be set under a Parlour, or lower chamber window. Then Pinks and Gilly-flowers, specially the matted Pink, and Clove Gilly-flower. Then the flowers of the Lime-tree. Then the Hony-suckles, so they be somewhat afar off. Of Bean-flowers I speak not, because they are field-flowers. But those which perfume the air most delightfully, not passed by as the rest, but being trodden upon and crushed, are three, that is, Burnet, Wild-time, and Water-Mints. Therefore you are to set whole alleys of them, to have the pleasure when you walk or tread.

For Gardens (speaking of those which are indeed prince-like, as we have done of Buildings) the contents ought not well to

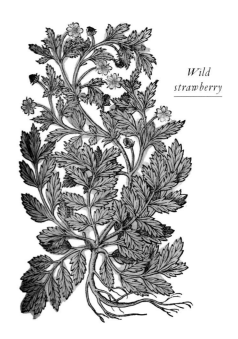

Wild strawberry

be under thirty acres of ground, and to be divided into three parts; a Green in the entrance, a Heath or Desart in the going forth, and the main Garden in the midst, besides alleys on both sides. And I like well, that four acres of ground be assigned to the Green, six to the Heath, four and four to either side, and twelve to the main Garden. The Green hath two pleasures; the one, because nothing is more pleasant to the eye than green grass kept finely shorn; the other, because it will give you a fair alley in the midst, by which you may go in front upon a stately hedg [hedge], which is to enclose the garden. But because the alley will be long, and in great heat of the year or day, you ought not to buy the shade in the Garden, by going in the sun through the Green; therefore you are of either side the Green to plant a covert alley upon carpenters work, about twelve foot in heighth, by which you may go in shade into the Garden. As for the making of knots of figures, with divers coloured earths, that they may lye under the windows of the house, on that side which the

Garden stands, they be but toys, you may see as good sights many times in tarts. The Garden is best to be square, encompassed on all the four sides with a stately arched hedg; the arches to be upon pillars of carpenters work, of some ten foot high, and six foot broad, and the spaces between of the same dimension with the breadth of the arch. Over the arches let there be an entire hedg, of some four foot high, framed also upon carpenters work, and upon the upper hedg, over every arch a little turret, with a belly, enough to receive a cage of birds; and over every space between the arches some other little figure, with broad plates of round coloured glass gilt, for the sun to play upon. But this hedg I intend to be raised upon a bank, not steep, but gently slope, of some six foot, set all with flowers. Also I understand, that this square of the Garden, should not be the whole breadth of the ground, but to leave on either side ground enough for diversity of side alleys, unto which the two covert alleys of the Green may deliver you; but there must be no alleys with hedges at either end of this great inclosure: not at the higher end, for letting your prospect upon this fair hedg from the Green; nor at the further end, for letting your prospect from the hedg through the arches upon the Heath. For the ordering of the ground within the great hedg, I leave it to variety of device. Advising nevertheless, that whatsoever form you cast it into; first it be not too busie, or full of work; wherein I, for my part, do not like images cut out in Juniper, or other garden-stuff, they be for children. Little low hedges, round like welts, with some pretty pyramids, I like well: and in some places fair columns upon frames of carpenters work. I would also have the alleys spacious and fair. You may have closer alleys upon the side grounds, but none in the main garden. I wish also in the very middle a fair mount, with three ascents and alleys, enough for four to walk abreast, which I would have to be perfect circles, without any bulwarks or imbosinents [embossments], and the whole

mount to be thirty foot high, and some fine banqueting house, with some chimneys neatly cast, and without too much glass.

For Fountains, they are a great beauty and refreshment, but Pools marr all, and make the Garden unwholsome, and full of flies and frogs. Fountains I intend to be of two natures, the one that sprinkleth or spouteth water, the other a fair receipt of water, of some thirty or forty foot square, but without fish, or slime, or mud. For the first, the ornaments of images gilt, or of marble, which are in use, do well; but the main matter is, so to convey the water, as it never stay, either in the bowls, or in the cistern, that the water be never by rest discoloured, green or red, or the like; or gather any mossiness or putrefaction. Besides that, it is to be cleansed every day by the hand; also some steps up to it, and some fine pavement about it doth well. As for the other kind of Fountain, which we may call a bathing-pool, it may admit much curiosity and beauty, wherewith we will not trouble ourselves; as that the bottom be finely paved, and with images, the sides likewise; and withal embellished with coloured

Stinking gladdon (iris)

Upright heartsease (violet)

glass, and such things of lustre; encompassed also with fine rails of low statues. But the main point is the same, which we mentioned in the former kind of Fountain, which is, that the water be in perpetual motion, fed by a water higher than the pool, and delivered into it by fair spouts, and then discharged away under ground, by some equality of bores, that it stay little. And for fine devices of arching water without spilling, and making it rise in several forms (of feathers, drinking-glasses, canopies, and the like) they be pretty things to look on, but nothing to health and sweetness.

For the Health [heath], which was the third part of our plot, I wish it to be framed, as much as may be, to a natural wildness. Trees I would have none in it, but some thickets made only of Sweet-Briar, and Hony-suckle, and some Wild Vine amongst, and the ground set with Violets, Strawberries and Primroses: for these are sweet and prosper in the shade. And these to be in the Heath, here and there, not in any order. I like

also little heaps, in the nature of mole-hills (such as are in wild-Heaths) to be set, some with Wild-Thyme, some with Pinks, some with Germander, that gives a good flower to the eye; some with Periwinckle, some with Violets, some with Strawberries, some with Couslips, some with Daizies, some with Red-Roses, some with Lilium Convallium [lily of the valley], some with Sweet-Williams red, some with Bears-Foot, and the like low flowers, being withal sweet and sightly. Part of which heaps, to be with standards, of little bushes, prickt upon their top, and part without; the standards to be Roses, Juniper, Holly, Bear-berries (but here and there, because of the smell of their blossom), Red Currans, Gooseberries, Rosemary, Bays, Sweet-Briar, and such like. But these standards to be kept with cutting, that they grow not out of course.

For the side grounds, you are to fill them with variety of alleys, private, to give a full shade, some of them, wheresoever the sun be. You are to frame some of them, likewise for shelter, that when the wind blows sharp, you may walk as in a gallery. And those

Purple garden violet

Detail from the title page of John Gerard's *The Herball*, 1633 edition

And God said, Behold, I have given you every herb bearing seed, which is upon the face of all the earth, and every tree, in the which is the fruit of a tree yielding seed; to you it shall be for meat.

GENESIS I.29–30

alleys must be likewise hedged at both ends, to keep out the wind, and these closer alleys must be ever finely gravelled, and no grass, because of going wet. In many of these alleys likewise, you are to set fruit trees of all sorts; as well upon the walls, as in ranges. And this would be generally observed, that the borders wherein you plant your fruit-trees, be fair and large, and low, and not steep, and set with fine flowers, but thin and sparingly, lest they deceive the trees. At the end of both the side grounds, I would have a mount of some pretty height, leaving the wall of the enclosure breast-high, to look abroad into the fields.

For the main Garden, I do not deny, but there should be some fair alleys ranged on both sides with fruit-trees, and some pretty tufts of fruit-trees and arbors with seats, set in some decent order; but these to be by no means set too thick; but to leave the main Garden so, as it be not close, but the air open and free; for as for shade I would have you rest upon the alleys of the side grounds, there to walk, if you be disposed, in the heat of the year or day: but to make account, that the main Garden is for the more temperate parts of the year; and in the heat of summer, for the morning, and the evening or over-cast days.

For Aviaries, I like them not, except they be of that largeness, as they may be turfed, and have living plants and bushes set in them, that the birds may have more scope,

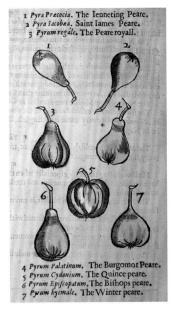

1 *Pyra Præcocia*. The Ienneting Peare.
2 *Pyra Iacobæa*. Saint Iames Peare.
3 *Pyrum regale*. The Peare royall.

4 *Pyrum Palatinum*. The Burgomot Peare.
5 *Pyrum Cydonium*. The Quince peare.
6 *Pyrum Episcopatum*. The Bishops peare.
7 *Pyrum hyemale*. The Winter peare.

Fruits of tame pear trees

Katherine pear tree

and natural neastling [nesting], and that no foulness appear in the floor of the aviary. So I have made a plat-form of a princely Garden, partly by precept, partly by drawing, not a model, but some general lines of it, and in this I have spared for no cost. But it is nothing, for great princes, that for the most part taking advice with work-men, with no less cost, set their things together, and sometimes add statua's [statues] and such things, for state and magnificence, but nothing to the true pleasure of a Garden.

Bakers ditch apple tree

English cherry tree

Province or
damask rose

The rose looks fair, but fairer we it deem
For that sweet odour which doth in it live.

SONNET 54

ACKNOWLEDGMENTS

In producing this book we are grateful for the assistance and support of Paul Edmondson, Emma Mulveagh, Jennifer Reid, Adam Sherratt, Andrew Thomas and the collections team at the Shakespeare Birthplace Trust; Rowena Alsey, Celia Falconer, Sarah Hull and Roger Thorp at Thames & Hudson; Caroline Brooke Johnson, Hannah Catterall, Roger Pringle and Sir Roy Strong.

The Shakespeare Birthplace Trust's collections can be viewed online at collections.shakespeare.org.uk

SOURCES OF ILLUSTRATIONS
a=above, c=centre, b=below

All pictures from the Shakespeare Birthplace Trust, other than © Sir John Soane's Museum. Title page, pages 34–35; © Rachel Pringle. Pages 98–99

Bacon, Francis, 'Of Gardens' in *The essays or counsels, civil and moral, of Sir Francis Bacon, Lord Verulam, Viscount St Alban* (London, 1680 edition). Page 101

Boydell, John and Josiah (publishers), *A Collection of prints from Pictures painted for the purpose of illustrating the Dramatic Works of Shakspeare by the Artists of Great Britain* (London, 1803). Vol. 1: pages 14, 22, 31, 58a; Vol. 2: pages 32–33a

Crane, Walter (illustrator), *Flowers from Shakespeare's Garden: a Posy from the Plays* (London, 1909 edition). Pages 38–39, 62, 64–65

Ellacombe, Henry Nicholson, *The Plant-Lore and Garden-Craft of Shakespeare* (London, 1896 edition). Pages 16–17, 42–43, 49, 50–53

First Folio, Mr. William Shakespeares Comedies, Histories, & Tragedies (London, 1623). Page 26

Gerard, John, *The Herball, or Generall Historie of Plantes,* (London, 1597 edition [monochrome],

and 1633 edition [contemporary hand-colouring]). Pages 10, 12, 15, 18, 32–33b, 45, 54–55, 66–67, 71, 74–75, 92–93, 96–97, 102–108, 112

Grindon, Leo H., *Shakspere Flora* (Manchester, 1883). Pages 41, 46–47, 78

Hill, Thomas, *The Gardeners Labyrinth* (London, 1577). Half title, pages 25, 27, 73, 76–77, 87a, 91

Law, Ernest, *Shakespeare's Garden, Stratford-upon-Avon* (London, 1922). Pages 11, 87b, 88–89

Lawson, William, *A New Orchard and Garden with The Country Housewife's Garden* (London, 1648 edition). Front cover, pages 25b, 69, 72a and b

Markham, Gervase, *The Second Book of the Countrie Farme: Of Gardens*, English translation from French by Richard Surflet (London, 1616). Pages 9, 19, 37, 42, 48, 56–57, 58b, 72c, 78, 90, 100

Postcards: 'Valentine views of Stratford upon Avon' by Valentine and Sons, Dundee. Pages 80–81

Rock Brothers and Payne (publishers), *Views of Stratford on Avon* (London 1864). Page 78

Singleton, Esther, *The Shakespeare Garden* (London, 1922 edition). Pages 94–95, 96

Songs of Shakespeare, Illuminated by H. C. Hoskyns Abrahall (London, 1866). Pages 36 (Illustration No. 15), 40 (Illustration No. 11)

Van de Passe, Crispijn, *Hortus Floridus* (Utrecht, 1614). Reproduced in Ellacombe, see above. Pages 49, 50–51

SOURCE OF SHAKESPEARE QUOTATIONS
Wells, Stanley, Gary Taylor, John Jowett and William Montgomery (eds), *The Oxford Shakespeare: The Complete Works* (Oxford, 2005, second edition)

INDEX